True Stories From Seattle

By

LAMONT CRANSTON

AuthorHouse™
1663 Liberty Drive
Bloomington, IN 47403
www.authorhouse.com
Phone: 1-800-839-8640

First published by AuthorHouse 12/1/2010

ISBN: 978-1-4520-8942-3 (e)
ISBN: 978-1-4520-8941-6 (sc)

Printed in the United States of America

This book is printed on acid-free paper.

SYNOPSIS

PREFACE: Introduces Seattle as a seacoast town with more than its share of nefarious charters.

INTRODUCTION: Lets the reader know that I was indicted and later convicted of "Mail and Wire Fraud Conspiracy" along with six other defendants. It was a precedent setting case. $228,000,000. Three years in a federal prison and its experiences opened a shadowy new world to me.

True Stories: Proceeds to introduce the myriad characters I met in prison and later after I paroled to Seattle. It details the names of the perpetrators of the crimes, the dates, how, and the wherefore of the crimes committed. It is a True Crime Drama.

DEDICATION

This is dedicated to all those who have become like little children.

Without the need of weapons, or any form of defense.

ACKNOWLEDGEMENT

I want to thank my friends that made this work possible. Without their help and encouragement, it would never have been accomplished. I extend my thanks to Linda Gravelle, Avard Wilson, Gary Rosquist, and Don Koler. I was amazed to find that we were still friends after it was a finished product.

I want to thank my enemies, too. If it had not been for them, I would have had nothing to write about.

I also want to extend my thanks to my personal detractors. They have a way of making me see things in Living Color, not just black and white. The plethora of their palette is a constant reminder to me that we forge our character in the fire of your own will. We just need to center ourselves and focus our attention properly.

To all the bad guys everywhere, I hope you get caught and punished. Then the world will be a safer and better place to live. I dedicate this work to the end that we may all become like children…Weaponless and without guile.

PREFACE

Seattle is a seacoast town. It is on the Pacific Rim and ships stuff all over the world. It is also the doorway to Alaska the last frontier. Because of the prominence Seattle plays in being a timber, mining, Micro-technology, plutonium producing place. A great variety of adventure seeking, wheeler-dealer nefarious players keep gracing the scene.

Some of these characters amass huge fortunes legitimately, but some of them operate on the fringe of legitimacy, or cross over into the heart of darkness and become full-fledged criminals. This book will deal with "Bad Guys", the crime-committing criminals who operate outside the law not because they have to, but because they choose to. They like the high stakes game of outwitting the cops and authorities. Sometimes they win.

And in spite of what you have been told "Crime does pay" if you are good at it. And some of these people are very, very good at crime. They reap handsome rewards from their activities over and over again. They keep playing the game until they are caught or killed. Usually they have to be killed. Anything short of killing them just delays them a little.

I am going to name names, dates, and places where these crimes were committed. My attorney says "this will get me dead", but since no one gets out of life alive I thought I would write it anyway. If your name is in here I apologize to you, but you shouldn't have done the crime. I hope you have to do the time. Maybe the good guys will get you and punish you.

INTRODUCTION

I paroled to Seattle in July 1981. I had just finished doing a stretch behind prison walls for the Federal Government also known as "Club Fed". I was indicted and convicted of "Mail and Wire Fraud Conspiracy" for $228,000,000. I didn't get the money but I got to do the time.

Everyone in the company was sent away. I got sentenced to forty-two months, the lightest sentence of any of the seven defendants. The trouble was it played out as a precedent setting case. Eight hundred forty three counts in the indictment and sixty-five thousand pages of sworn testimony. It made a train wreck of our lives.

I was offered immunity by Charles Turner the prosecuting attorney if I would incriminate everyone else in the company including myself. I refused the deal and the rest is history. (Smile) It was the first time the government didn't have to separate the defendants and have separate trials.

Because the government prevailed it has since become established law.

I never took the stand or said a word in my own defense upon the advice of my court appointed attorney. I was too dumb to figure out Susan Reese was working for the government, not for me. I lost my wife, my kids, my friends, and got myself kicked out of my church in the next ninety days. What an eye opener. In the words of modern day evangelists "I had an epiphany, I was born again." (Smile) They took everything away from me but my sense of humor. I refused to give that up. I'm sure our forefathers and the framers of the Constitution of the United States meant to include a sense of humor as a God given inalienable right. Mine has stood me in good stead and kept me semi-sane throughout what some would term an ordeal. I perceive it more as an odyssey. In light of the Enron scandal and other huge cases being played out in today's newspapers ours was chump change. Just pop bottle money.

PAST HISTORY

I was born on an Indian reservation in Montana in 1938. My mom was named Hazel and she was a full-blooded Indian. I never met my dad but he must have been white. Cuz I'm what Indians call a passer, I look white. That means I could go into the reservation store that had a sign: "Only two Indians in the store at a time" and buy Coca-Cola and the proprietor would not kick me out because he thought I was white. The rule on the reservation was "If you are black get back. If you are brown hang around. If you are white you are right." I wanted to be white. My mom had seventeen children, some lived and some died. The State took most of them.

I was living in a little trailer on the reservation with my two older brothers when my mom poisoned the man living with us to death. We got locked in with him while he died. She put a padlock on the outside the trailer and a do not disturb sign on the door. I was four years old.

We were Spam in a can. Eventually the cops busted us out. She went to prison. We went to the orphanage; also known as the used baby store.

I'm afraid we live in a disposable society. We throw people away from us. The very old, and the very young that we don't want we just dispose of them. It has become a very profitable industry. I now joke about the fact the White man can turn anything into a profitable business opportunity i.e. Living, dying, and everything in between. (Smile.)

In 1938 it wasn't fashionable to adopt Indian boys. Now it's popular to do so. I encourage people to have an Indian for a pet, or take an Indian to lunch, etc. Federal Law says you can test-drive an Indian orphan without formally adopting them for six months. You must provide food, clothing and shelter. There are no Federal standards for quality.

In the 1940's no one in their right mind wanted to adopt three little Indian boys. The rule of thumb to get adopted was you had to be adopted by the time you were seven years old or nobody would have you. To help us be more marketable the orphanage split us up and told each of us that our brothers were killed in a car crash. It must have worked because we got borrowed and returned a few times then someone adopted a couple of us.

The court produced new birth certificates, changed our names, and sealed everything else away. It took thirty-one years and many trips to Montana but with enough court orders I found my brothers. The trouble was too much time had elapsed and they had new identities. They were legitimized into White mainstream society and they didn't want to remember the past or be found. White European society is truly powerful. It absorbs every other culture. They disappear into the maw of its oneness. Since the written word is the only authority really recognized the "White Mans Paper" is all-powerful.

Two White people adopted me. Even their last name was White, Alan and Hazel. We moved to California. Hazel couldn't have kids. They had met on a blind date and got married one month later. Neither had ever dated before. She had eleven brothers and sisters. She was neurotic and an over communicator. Alan's dad had died when he was seven years old. His mother worked at Sears with her old maid sister. She brought sailors home at night and hit the bars regularly. As a consequence he was taciturn and uncommunicative. After we moved to California, thirteen years later I joined the Air Force. In that thirteen years I never saw them kiss, hold hands, or express affection for each other. I do not know to this day if they liked each other. They are dead now so that chapter is long closed. But they helped me find my Mantra, "Anything that doesn't kill you will make you stronger." (Smile)

Since I didn't drink, do drugs, or smoke I had good experiences in the military, I was never a skirt chaser so I got spared the pangs and angst of falling in love. Instead I met the Mormons. They thought I was an ideal candidate for their church. I eliminated myself forthwith and with great alacrity disabused them of that notion immediately. Until, they professed to have a living prophet in Salt Lake City Utah. It intrigued me so I rented an airplane and flew to meet their prophet. It was the most profound experience I have ever had in my whole lifetime. He invited me in. He spoke of my past without my telling him as though he had personally lived it. He so uncannily predicted my future that I only had to follow the tracks in the snow. I became a Latter Day Saint and devoutly followed their teachings and doctrine. Who would have guessed I would marry a Mormon dairy princess from Idaho, with a mother named Hazel. We produced three kids (who remain incommunicado) to this day. And we moved on.

Flashback: In an effort to live the American dream I worked two jobs every summer to go to college and earn a passport to happiness. I perceived that paper could open doors that would otherwise remain closed to me. I found my formal education was enlightening and rewarding but not all encompassing. Nevertheless it got me my job as a finance mortgage broker with a national company. I became their general manager and chief executive officer reporting to the president. I flew 2,000,000 air miles per year. We did business worldwide. I made a good living and we were happy. For a dumb Indian boy off a reservation in Montana things couldn't be better.

Then a cop knocked on my door and the world turned upside down. It seemed like the sky was falling right on me. Everything went into slow motion and dragged on interminably until sentencing. After that a blur and I was wafted into a new dimension. I met people I never knew existed except on T.V. and the movies. Reality eclipsed fantasy. Let me introduce you to the nether world of the "bad guys".

TRUE STORIES

The wife and kids left the day after I got sentenced. I expected it to happen. So it didn't come as a complete surprise. I offered to share my cell with them but my wife didn't like the way she looked in stripes. So I put them on the big silver bird to Idaho. They were as jubilant as the children of Israel going into the Promised Land. When you get sentenced, the judge makes you declare whether or not you are going to appeal your sentence. You have two years to do so. I opted to get it over with. I got the courts permission to go to California to work, knowing the Mounties always get their man. I knew the U.S. Marshals would be along to pick me up and transport me to the 10,000 Chinese hells at any time. Mark Twain said, "Nothing so sobers and focuses the human mind as knowing you are going be hung in the morning," Especially when they erect the scaffold outside your jail window.

I got arrested at work in Pasadena. Two undercover cops in Hawaiian shirts took me into custody and transported me to Los Angeles central jail. Fifteen hundred men a day are arrested in Los Angeles every day. You haven't lived until you see one hundred ninety buses transporting handcuffed prisoners in chains to court each day. Just strip-searching, de-lousing you, and assigning you takes seven to eight hours. When they drop kick you into a cell with five other guys, bunks stacked three high on two sides of a ten by twelve steel cage, you get the message you aren't being sent there for being good.

You have to wear colored plastic bracelets. Red ones are keep away- murderers only. Blue ones are drugs slick and dangerous guys. Yellow ones are low risk general population. White is protective custody, snitches, and sex offenders, usually pederasts that prey on children. Inside they refer to them as "Having Short Eyes." They only see children as prey and cannot be cured in spite of what you hear to the contrary. They are sick forever! They immediately find God, get religion and skate free, only a bullet finally stops them.

They held me in the Los Angeles jail for six weeks waiting for the marshals to come and take me to McNeil Island penitentiary. McNeil was at that time a maximum-security prison. Murderers were housed on the ground floor; everyone else was stacked up to ten tiers high. Each tier was ten feet above the other. I got to be ninety feet above the floor. I was housed with five other guys in a twenty five by thirty foot cell. I thought I was moving on up to the Eastside.

Outside they had guard towers with machine guns and thirty caliber rifles to shoot you off the fence if you tried to escape. The concertina wire on the top of the fence would slash you to ribbons if you tried to climb over it. They didn't put up steel shutters on the windows when you ate, like they did in Los Angeles. The shutters were so if they had to shoot you during the meal no bullets or pellets from the shotguns would go outside. That sometimes put a damper on partaking of their excellent cuisine. Marching with one shoulder against the wall with no talking reminded me of my early military training. At McNeil they patted you down in the corridor and only one tier at a time could eat, but looking out the windows made the food taste better. Until I saw one man killed for a candy bar. Then I reprioritized my values. Human life wasn't highly regarded there.

They soon downgraded the prison. The baddest men got sent elsewhere. Then I became a trustee. That opened up the windows of heaven to me. I was paid nine cents per hour to work in the prison hospital for an alcoholic psychiatrist. Most men only got seven cents per hour. I was now upper class. The psychiatrist was a little kinky. She liked bare bottom spankings and bank robbers. She got one of them out early and bought him an airplane. His name was Dennis. He went to live with her in her mansion in

Silverdale.   They would still be together but Dennis robbed her bank and flew away to Las Vegas with all the money. He spent the money on hookers and gambling. He didn't win! The F.B.I. was very angry with her...but she had more "Juice" than they did. So she walked free.

SRO THEATRES

Barbara the psychiatrist had some issues of her own to deal with. She adopted a thirteen-year-old bad girl. The girl and the doctors' tugboat captain husband succumbed to the lures of the flesh. She caught them a couple of times doing the nasty together, so she put choke collars and a short leash on both of them. She exacted promises from each of them under oath, but eventually the forbidden fruit was too powerful and sweet so they ran away together. Stolen fruit is always the sweetest. The next chapter got even weirder than the first.

She then adopted a nineteen-year-old retarded boy named Robert. He was strong as an ox, but had the mental capacity of a seven year old, maybe less. On Halloween day he spotted the next-door neighbor's son and some strange men unloading twenty-two tons of Marijuana on their beach. He went down to investigate. Everyone pulled their guns and wanted to waste him. The neighbor's son reassured the bad men that he would keep Robert busy. They went up to the house to play cards. The men on the beach unloaded Robert Sterling's grass and hid it from sight. They then boarded the rented yacht and sailed away.

The SRO Theatres "Sterling Recreational Organization" had just made a major score in their new entertainment enterprise. The only thing is, they didn't realize how badly they traumatized Robert. He went upstairs and got his mother's sedatives. He fed them to the neighbor's son. When he became sleepy Robert let him lie down on one of the beds upstairs. After he was sound asleep, he got his mother's gun and blew the guy's brains all over the walls. When the cops came to investigate that night, all the power was out.   Robert was sitting under the piano downstairs, humming to himself in the dark. The cop told me "searching that house by flashlight on Halloween night was the worst case he'd ever been on." Robert is at Western State Hospital.

His porch light doesn't just flicker; it's all the way out. Nobody's home.

PRISON PSYCHOLOGY

Dr. Thompson was McNeil Islands prison psychologist. He was doing his P.H.D. on the postulate that criminals have weak minds and are born that way. In his efforts to test his hypothesis, he invented a cigarette machine with flashing lights and buzzers. If you could figure out a sequence of flashing lights the machine paid anywhere from one to three cigarettes. He kept a statistical log of how many men tried and failed. I let it be known that even though I didn't smoke, I liked zam-zams and whoom-whooms. This is a generic prison term for snacks i.e. candy, chips, cookies, soda pop. All of which has to be purchased with credits at the company store, the prison commissary. The word went out to the general population! I had worked in Cryptography for the Air Farce. The men fronted me credits to figure out the patterns. I then copied the patterns down and sold copies to everyone that wanted to beat the machine and Dr. Thompson. By the time he figured out that he was beaten badly, he had to pay out over two hundred cartons of cigarettes.

Dr. Thompson liked to run marathons. We had a little black bank robber named James Short from South Carolina that was a vegetarian. I had people look out for his needs. He ran twenty miles a day, seven days a week. But he had to flatten a twenty-year sentence for robbing a white bank and making a black man lie on top of a white teller.

We also had a dentist that was riding a D.E.A beef for writing too may scripts. His girlfriend turned him in for not giving her Quaaludes and she burned his clothes in the snow, and then called the I.R.S. on him. He could run like the eight million dollar man. I never saw a human being that could run fifty-five marathons over thirty years and always finish. I went to the warden and recommended Dr. Bob Layman to be a trustee. He had five kids who moved from Alaska to be near their dad. He was a good hearted and kind man.

RUNNING WITH THE BULLS

Meanwhile, Dr. Thompson had a new postulate. No criminal had the necessary drive to win a marathon because they were all quitters and losers. One thousand two hundred twenty incarcerated felons were quite outraged that they would never get a chance to prove the doctor wrong. He wouldn't accept the challenge of racing behind prison walls. He said "it depressed his spirit, so he couldn't run his best!" But, he would race any man that had been incarcerated outside prison walls for the Tacoma marathon, and furthermore he would prove that any man that "fell" (a prison term for being arrested) lacked the heart to finish anything worthwhile.

With this I went to the warden. He said, "If you can get guards to transport you, and sponsors to sponsor you, I will let two men run in that race!" We had our two men. Every day they ran their hearts out. The prisoners gave them their food and encouraged them.

Then the rest of us went to work. The men would stop Dr. Thompson and ask him how he felt. How were his workouts going? Did he feel okay? He seemed stressed, looked weak or pale. Soon, he got sick. He suffered from general malaise and stomach upsets. The day of the race was cold and windy. The rest is history. The two prisoners finished one and two. Dr. Thompson never finished. He hit the wall at thirteen miles, slunk to his car and drove quietly away. He later had himself transferred to another prison in Texas. Cést Lavie.

HARRISON AND THE GOON SQUAD

Castro dumped eight hundred prisoners on our shores. He got rid of his Cuban malefactors by shipping them to us. We were inundated. The feds said they weren't really in prison. Immigration Naturalization Service (I.N.S) said, "They were as at the door waiting for entrance." Meanwhile the Feds made them work, but wouldn't give them any necessities, soap, toothpaste, clean clothes etc. I wrote a "writ" to Judge Jack Tanner in Tacoma and he had it corrected but it took time.

Meanwhile, Harrison the huge guard that ran the goon squad and was a high ranking Mason would go into their cells at night and beat them with his fists and a baton, just for the fun of it. He was unstoppable. Harrison stole sixty-five cows and had the inmates butcher them. He then sold the meat in Tacoma. He ran a trap line from the prison farm on the island and sold the pelts, even though the island is a protected wildlife sanctuary.

Harrison was a six foot eight inch three hundred forty pound sadist. He knew nobody dared to stop or prosecute him. He was a law unto himself. He even raped a couple of the other officer's wives and got away with it. Not everyone behind walls is there by court order. The warden got drunk and punched a woman in an elevator in town. He had to go to jail on the weekends. Then he got in a family fight and banned his wife and kids from the island. What a hoot.

When the fox is watching the chicken coop and you cannot tell the players apart, except from their uniforms, it's a good thing justice is blind. There is a saying on the street. "If you want the law, go to court. If you want justice, wait until you die."

RUSSIAN DIAMONDS

I met Chris Boyce of the "Falcon and the Snowman" fame. Someone inadvertently left a twenty-foot ladder by the wall and he escaped. They caught him later in a diner in Bellingham, Washington. Three hundred armed lawmen surrounded the diner with drawn guns and yelled "Drop that hamburger Boyce, you're under arrest". He sold our K-11 satellite secrets to the Soviets before our government could give them to them. He is doing life for treason. His dad was embarrassed because he was in charge of security for TRW.

I also did time with Stanley Rifkin who stole Fourteen million dollars from Security Pacific Bank. He rounded off all checks with odd cents and funneled them into a dummy account he created for himself. He got away undetected.

But lust took over and he remembered a girl that worked with him as a vault teller with a perfect ass. He invited miss perfect buns to lunch at Denny's.   He let her choose one of the diamonds he bought from the Russians with the bank's stolen money.   She went straight to the F.B.I. (fumbling bunch of idiots).   They set up the Four Seasons Hotels.   Stanley and miss cheeky arrived not knowing everyone in the hotel was F.B.I. except them.   Stanley and hot buns were there to do another deal with the Russians.   She was hot for the plot!

When the deal went down, according to Stanley, the F.B.I. came out of the walls, the floors, and the chandelier, everywhere.   Miss perfect buns walked free.   Stanley is in Lompoc Prison Camp in California.   The bank and the state of California claimed the money.   The state said "The bank didn't know the money was missing, they aren't going to give it back to the depositors because they don't know who they were."   The bank got a judge to give them a friendly nod.   The money disappeared again. Stanley has a new computer program worked out that will steal more money than last time. Some folks are slow learners.

NO ONE IS IMMUNE

Sometimes even attorneys get caught by the very law they profess to represent. I met a neat handsome attorney behind prison walls. He represented drug dealers. He never lost a case. The Feds turned a drug dealer. They set the attorney up by getting the dealer to make an appointment on a bogus case they trumped up. When the dealer left, he asked if he could leave some valuables in Gordon's safe. Over the weekend the cops came in with a warrant. Heroin and cocaine put the attorney away. His client walked free. Gordon is planning a "get back."

You can't rescue people from themselves. Most people behind walls belong there. I only met a very few men that I believed were truly innocent of wrongdoing. Most malefactors have a continual pattern of mis-behavior. The majority lack perspective. They cannot link cause and effect. Fortunately, I have met very few truly evil men. Most people lack the focus to corrupt

27

everyone around them to despoil everything of true value. But I did meet a few unrepentant worthless throw away personalities with no social or redeeming value. They should never be released.

If I were to change the prison system, I would have ten prisons in very remote areas. All murderers would be locked up together, all druggers in another, thieves all together, and all the rapists together. No mixing or co-mingling. They should put them deep underground. If they escaped, it would be too remote to get very far away. They would be easy to apprehend and they wouldn't pose an immediate threat to society.

Right now all we have is a crime college. All attorneys should be assigned their cases. They shouldn't get to pick them. A general fund should pay their set fees, i.e. $1,000 for each case no matter how long it takes. This would ensure a fast and speedy trial. Justice would be better served and soon the word would get out that there is no mileage in delay. A first offence would get one month in jail and community service. A second offence would get six months in jail. Punishment for the third offence would be one year in jail. Anything more than two years in jail serves as a dis-incentive. It creates resentment, not remorse for wrongful behavior. I would put career criminals in prison for ten years, twenty years and life. No mitigating circumstances. You do the crime. You do the time.

The war against drugs is not happening. What a joke! Fourteen percent of the population is dysfunctional because of drugs. As long as someone with no experience or education can make ten thousand percent profit on their money and the demand exceeds the supply, nothing is going to stop the drug trade. The government is getting a paycheck for doing nothing but putting on a good show. Stop the suppliers! Destroy the cash crop! Forget the users. You can't catch and jail all the users. There aren't enough jails on this planet to house everybody. Anyone that tells you differently is pumping sunshine up your pants. Billions of dollars are being wasted. Find the dealers, execute them, or lock them up for twenty years. That will slow them and stop them. You have to raise the stakes. Call it punishment not correction. To kill a snake, you cut off the head and the body dies. Nothing else works!

The most profitable business in the world is war. The next most profitable is oil, if you are wired into one of the four sources that control oil. The next most profitable business is drugs, ethical and unethical. The next is unified religions collectively. Then diamonds.

CRIME PAYS

The United States of America is the largest weapon maker and distributor in the world. It is therefore inevitable that there will be wars. John Maynard Keynes the greatest economist that ever lived defined business as "the maximization of profit without regards to people" you can't say it any better. (Smile)

I had a client that published a newspaper called "The Good News". He went bankrupt. Take the profit out of crime if you want to make it untenable.

While behind walls I met a bank robber. Dale held up at least twenty-seven banks that I know of. Most robbers are just stick up men, they hold up tellers and get about seven thousand five hundred dollars. They are sentenced to eight years. They serve one third of that, two years and eight months, then they are set free to be stupid again. Dale was never caught. After nineteen years of holding up vaults and twenty

31

seven million dollars the F.B.I. gave up. They framed him for a bank he didn't rob and got him sentenced to twenty years. They never recovered a dime. He did the time. With one million four hundred twenty one thousand dollars per year, they didn't discourage him. The money was insured with your tax dollars. Dale calculated it as an acceptable business cost, a worthwhile trade off to realize long-term success.

The banks don't want you to know that employees steal the real big money internally. If you knew that, you wouldn't trust them with your money. There are so many people dipping the till internally that even the federal and state oversight regulation can't stop it. Fourteen banks a day are robbed externally in the United States, but the real money evaporates on the week ends while the bank is technically insolvent awaiting Monday's opening to balance the books again.

There is no rehabilitation in prison. Just angry men in cages. Rehabilitation comes from the Latin rehabare: to reinvest dignity or restore dignity. You cannot restore that which never existed. Prison is about punishment and failure. Any psychologist can tell you the sooner the punishment follows the act of inappropriate behavior, the sooner you extinguish the bad behavior. Also, the punishment should be in direct proportion to fit the crime. The system does just the opposite. That is why the recidivism rates are so high in the United States.

Sweden has the best rehabilitation rate in the world with a very low crime rate, and one of the highest standards of living worldwide. When you are in violation of the law in Sweden, they arrest you, try you quickly, and make you meet your victims in court, Assess damage to the law, sentence you appropriately, and give you a job in their automobile plants, or other prison industries. You earn money at half the rate of other employees. You can have a bank account and family can visit you readily. You must reimburse those wronged with the money you earned. You pay your debt to society gainfully employed. Your focus is on earning your freedom and paying back those you wronged. When your sentence is completed you can remain working for Viggen, Volvo, Saab, or whoever employs you, and you are eligible for a raise and have pride and dignity restored. You have acknowledged your error, paid your debt to society and moved on. This is true rehabilitation.

POLICE HUMOR

In prison everyone orchestrates his demand with threats. Move, or I'll kill you! Pass the salt, or I'll kill you! Give me that, or I'll kill you! It is the ultimate threat, even the cops use it. When they transport you, you are handcuffed, and leg chains are put on you along with a belly chain that is fastened to you and nineteen other men. Boarding the bus is loads of fun. After you are loaded and seated the cop boards the bus and arms his shotgun. It is loaded with double 00 buckshot that will blow you to pieces or cut you in half. He then tells the one good joke he knows deadpan faced, "I hope nobody here has got rabbit in them cuz I'd hate to have to kill you". When I'd raise my hand and ask, "if you shot us in the bus wouldn't some of those pellets ricochet around and get you too?" The men would laugh, but the officers would get real mad. If you don't have two or three death threats by noon, it's going to be a slow day. (Smile) Oh well, some people would complain if they were hung with a new rope.

SOLITARY

Someone put some goldfish in the punch dispenser in the chow hall. You would have thought their food was poisoned by they way the inmates reacted. They blamed the cops and filed writs that they were subject to cruel and unusual punishment. The cops locked everybody in their cells and did a general shakedown. They found guns, knives, drugs, and my big Hershey Bar with almonds. It was contraband, so they put me in the hole, i.e. solitary confinement for ten days. While you are in the hole, it is semi dark. Only one light bulb lights the corridor between the cages. You are put in a strip cell with no bedding. A metal tray is welded to the wall with a thin mattress and no blankets. Most men get sick, cold, depressed, and unhappy so they capitulate.

While you're in the hole you talk to each other by calling out. Hey A-9 this is B-10, "What are you in for?" While in the hole for my evil Hershey bar caper the Marshall's brought in a guy in transit named Woody. As a Marshall's holdover, he would be gone the next day. "Hey guys, this is Woody in C-5, Who wants to make a hundred bucks? I have ten million in bearer bonds in the trunk of my Cadillac. It's bad paper I printed the bonds myself! How do I make them disappear?"

I was in cell 2B. 2B or not 2B. "How do I get paid?" I queried.

"I'll have my girlfriend put it on your books!" he said. I reached out to a guy who owed me a favor. The bonds went away. So did Woody. The F.B.I. let his girl friend drive the car away without searching the trunk of the car. No wonder they can't find four hundred missing handguns and three hundred missing computers.

For the money spent nobody catches more crooks than America's Most Wanted. Walsh and the television are an unbeatable pair. That is the highest and best use, of a resource. We need more dedicated crime fighters. We need to enlist the public's help in opposing crime and fighting evil. Just throwing more money to hire more police is not a tenable solution.

We need moms and dads to stay together. We need family structure. Most children have a work ethic by the time they are four years old, or they don't get one. The school or the church cannot replace the influence of the parents. In the words of Porsche motor cars, "Accept no substitute." We need new tax laws that favor two parent families, and I don't mean same sex parents. We need encouragement and incentives to cause people to choose marriage over just living together. If we have to pay for something good, to have it, as opposed to not having it, we should do so. In the words of the education bumper sticker, "If you think education is expensive, you should try ignorance."

If everyone paid a fair income tax, i.e. ten percent across the board there would be plenty of money to pay for it and people would be more willing to pay their share. It would level the playing field. Stop the cheating and lying from the government, and the people will lessen their dishonesty. Most people want to do the right thing; they have just lost their way. We need to have renewed hope set for us by the leaders of the people, not as Will Rogers joked, "the best politicians money will buy!" Albert Schweitzer said, "The three things most important to helping people to change are example, example, example."

In some ways, prison is the most orderly place you will ever live in. Jail is not. Jail has mostly young dangerous players who are trying to prove they are tougher, smarter, quicker, and more ruthless then everyone else. Prison has mostly long term, full time residents that are resigned to being caught. Because of the overcrowding, everyone is a little paranoid. When you bump against a guy, you let him see your empty hands and tell him, "Hey brother, I'm sorry, it was an accident. Nothing was intended." Otherwise, he will dwell on the incident, decide you are out to get him, and he will torch you in your sleep, or stab you. Once you see a man doused with a flammable liquid and turned into a living Ronsen lighter, you realize the cops can't help or stop it in time. Most everyone carries a weapon, usually a shank. Any metal can be rubbed on cement until it's razor sharp.

ZANE

There are only two ways to die. You stop breathing or your heart stops beating. Three buttons down on a mans shirt, regardless of his size will stop a mans heart. So you stay alert to the guy that drifts toward you from the side. He is the one who will step inside and in one dexterous move shove the sharpened metal in and twist so a hole is torn in the pericardial sac. You are technically dead by the time you hit the ground. Everyone will just keep walking. No one sticks around to answer any questions or watch; it's a done deal. It's game over for you.

Most people buddy up. They join the Crips, the Bloods, the Blacks, the Indians, or the Latinos. They all try to recruit you. The Neo-Nazis are the most hated by all. I resisted recruitment. I explained that when the man in the black dress lowered the gavel on me, they didn't offer to help me, or serve my time. So I was doing my time and nobody else's. They didn't thank me for sharing, or anything, but it let me keep my own space. You either stand up for something, or you will lie down for everything.

Zane, a three hundred pound Nazi skinhead was stabbed to death by a one hundred thirty five pound Mexican, he scared too badly. Zane dominated the weight room. He bench-pressed five hundred pounds. He had killed two guys and ground them into dog food. Everyone with a brain deferred to him. He ran the prison inside. But he humiliated the new guy and told him he was going to come into his cell at night and rape him and make him his girlfriend. It so traumatized the new guy that he took off running. When the evening meal rolled around Victor waited for Zane on the staircase. Victor was five feet six inches tall. Zane was six feet ten inches tall. Seventy five percent of a man's weight is from his waist up. Victor knew this. When he ran up the stairs toward Zane, everyone gave him room; they thought he had snapped and had a death wish. Trying to reach down for Victor made

44

Zane's body weight shift forward. He over reached himself. He was top heavy. He was dead before he finished falling. No one mourned for Zane, not even the remaining Nazis. Everyone had moved up one notch on the food chain.

SELLING A PRISON

My time was up at McNeil Island Penitentiary. The Federal Government decided to screw the State of Washington. They sold the prison to the state! If it weren't so comical, it would have been tragic. Dixie Lee Ray sent some really razor sharp dudes over to survey, and do an on-site-inspection of the property. I was asked to escort them around the island along with the assistant warden and some burly cops. My instructions were "Shut your mouth unless we ask you something. Don't volunteer anything." I could do that. It was why I was a trustee. Well the Feds gave the state the old razzle-dazzle. They made a dollar twenty-five and mirrors look like one hundred million dollars. We marched those boys in circles. The Feds pretended they were a bunch of country boys that just fell off the turnip truck and rolled into town.

After (Scoop) Senator Jackson put this state on the map by brokering a deal with the

Atomic Energy Commission, he let them secretly build and house a facility that was the U.S. counterpart of Chernobyl, Russia, a really nice Uranium enrichment plant coupled with a very lovely Plutonium breeder reactor. All were within a few hundred yards of the Columbia River, talk about poisoning the well everybody drinks out of. (smile)

Anyway, the Feds locked the prisoners in their cages while bulldozers on the far side of the island dug trenches ten feet deep. Inside those trenches, they buried thousands of cases of food purchased in Viet Nam. It was the food the taxpayers paid twice for, that the Federal Government was feeding to us in prison. Well the rest is history.

Dixie Lee Ray, the retired governor, had one last favor to pay so she could live out the rest of her life in seclusion on her Fox Island retreat. She had to convince the State of Washington to buy McNeil Island penitentiary. She did her job! Just like she did when she was selected by presidential appointment to be the head of the Atomic Energy Commission years earlier. She allowed huge underground cisterns of used radioactive material to be stored in Washington State.

Richland Washington, also known as radioactive city, is probably the most poisonous place on earth. We have more stored Plutonium there than anywhere else on this orb. Plutonium is the most poisonous substance known to man. Twenty ounces of it airborne is enough to kill every living human being on the planet. We have lost track of more than four hundred pounds of this green Kryptonite. In addition to that, we have hundreds of thousands of gallons of that stuff buried in the ground within a few hundred yards of the Columbia River. But, "it is okay, don't worry!" The government says so! Even Kerr McGee, that built the reactors that leak, says, "Don't worry. We have their solemn word everything is alright." While even as I write these words, our cowboy skull and cross bones president wants to attack

Iraq because they might have something deadly that could hurt us. "Weapons of mass destruction."

When McNeil Island closed I got transferred to Lompoc, California prison camp. I got to ride the Greyhound bus to my next place of incarceration. It was cool to lie back on the loping dog and see the world go by. When I got to Lompoc, I was in for the shock of my life. Guys wore their own clothes. They housed you in dorms with partitioning cubicles. They served the food cafeteria style. You only went to work if you wanted to. You could pay an inmate to do your job if you didn't feel like working. You could work in the furniture factory for sixteen cents per hour, making desks, and in and out boxes for judges. The irony of which was not lost on me. (Smile)

I took a job immediately. Guys carried cash, gambled, sold drugs, ran gangs, but there were no fences apparently. I soon learned things are often not as they appear to be in this life. Life is uncertain; you better learn to eat your dessert first. Motion detectors buried in the ground on the perimeter of the camp caught more than one walk away that thought he could take a bush furlough. Going behind the bushes and just keep walking didn't work there.   Most never saw the hidden T.V. cameras in the trees with the telephoto lenses until too late, when they were surrounded by angry cops with drawn guns.

OLD CRIME PARTNERS

When I reported to the furniture factory, lo and behold, the person in charge was a guy I knew, an inmate named Jerry Lutz. He was one of my fall partners. That is a prison term for someone sentenced with you. Generally the Feds never let two guys from the same crime conviction go to the same facility. There might be hard feelings and someone could get killed. The Federal compact contract that the Feds operate under reads: The Federal Government agrees to transport and house the defendant in a reasonable manner, using reasonable caution in warehousing their body so as not to deliberately expose them to unnecessary or unreasonable risk. i.e. not to deliberately put them in harms way.

When Jerry Lutz, the Vice President of Nationwide Funding and founding partner of the corporation saw me, he was so pale and shaken I thought he would pass out. He started gasping and noisily sucking in air. I didn't know then that he had run off with Jack Stewart's wife. Nor did I know he had paid cash for a new condominium next to the prison camp. He also had a new dove gray Lincoln Continental he paid cash for. Lois came to visit him in that car every visiting day. They had a boat and other expensive toys. It seems Jack, the president, got sick and was hospitalized. The doctors thought Jack would die. So did Jerry and Lois! They seized the company checkbook and all the funds and ran off together.

The next thing I knew two big guards came and handcuffed me at work and took me to the warden's office. The warden was very angry. "You didn't tell me you had enemies here!" he exclaimed vehemently. With lots of pejoratives, and vituperous words thrown in, he made his point.

"I wasn't shown a guest list when I arrived here; I didn't know he was here," I answered.

The warden said "I should put you in the hole for this."

"I've been there before; it ain't nothing;" I replied.

He then said, "I might just transfer your ass."

I answered, "I was looking for a home when I came here; it doesn't matter which cage I serve my time in."

It seems Jerry ran to the warden and asked for protective custody. I thought it was extremely funny. It was a tempest in a teacup as the British are fond of saying.

BUSINESS INSIDE PRISON

Life settled down again and I went about my business. I worked in the prison library, the furniture shop, and I signed up one thousand one hundred men to write to lonely women. Things were humming merrily along when the warden had me cuffed and brought into his office again. It seemed he felt it was wrong for me to charge the men five bucks each to write to women.

He said, "It was illegal to run a business behind prison walls while incarcerated." I pointed out quite accurately and succinctly that there was no statute presently on the books that specifically prohibited me from doing so. Challenge Ministries had contracts with the bureau of prisons and operated quite successfully. That in point of fact, the prison commissary was operating illegally then.

Every time the Feds move you from one facility to another and book you into the new facility, they take your shorts, toothpowder, razor, and shaving cream. They declare it as contraband and make you buy new items from their company store. I thought he was going to have apoplexy. I had no idea a human beings neck veins could distend that far without rupturing. He was yelling so loud I believe he could wake the dead. He seemed upset. Well, the upshot of all that was he closed me down, but not before everybody in my coterie of lonely men "Pen Pals" had a lady to write to. It seems that ladies like outlaws.

I found out the kitchen door couldn't be locked at night. What a Godsend! I went into prison weighing one hundred sixty pounds. Some prison chefs must have left a master cookbook they all cook from-a legacy of fat if you will, the Martha Stewart of incarcerated felons. They had at least twenty two hundred recipes for cooking starch. I had ballooned to two hundred eighty six pounds.

The cops love this because they know fat guys can't run fast. They move slower and are less dangerous. Between the saltpeter in your food and the fat, the testosterone level falls way down and their job is less difficult and dangerous. That was okay with me.

I discovered more people eat out of boredom than hunger, at least in America. Prison is no exception to that rule. All those heavenly treats were just waiting for me to come and liberate them. I soon learned if I trundled them around to the dorms, everybody would pay me a buck for a late night snack. The prison just threw the stuff away, or fed it to the hogs down on the pig farm. I figured as a future farmer of America, my pigs came first.

Like all good things, nothing lasts forever. One night I went down to the chow hall and slipped quietly inside; I heard voices. That was a bad thing. I figured I was busted, but instead, it was just two Nazi dudes trying to hold a large black man down so they could cut off his thumbs with a butcher knife. Well, some stuff doesn't need an explanation. They were interfering with our right to make a living. Between the two of us, we leveled the playing field. Just because a guy shaves his hair, cops an attitude, and carves a swastika in his forehead doesn't make him right. In my mind he is not the sharpest tool in the toolbox. Larry felt the same way. After we got rid of Hitler's' boys, we had a feast. From then on I had a new business partner. Life was sweet once again.

Shakespeare wrote, "Tomorrow, tomorrow, and tomorrow creeps by in its petty pace from day to day until the last syllable of recorded time and all of today's yesterdays are just drops that drip into that great pool of forgetfulness." He must have known about prison. No one else has ever described it better.

MINI-PRISONS

I GOT BORED. So I secured a one-gallon pickle bottle with a lid. Lompoc had the biggest, meanest red ants I had ever seen. I dug up their hole. I captured their queen and hundreds of soldier ant workers. I incarcerated them in my pickle bottle with lots of loose earth so they could dig a new village. I put them in my cubicle, fed them every day and watched them endlessly.

One day the cops did a surprise inspection. They caught me with my ants. They said that they were contraband. They asked me what I was doing with them? I explained that I was playing prison warden and prisoners with them. The one kind of twisted ant was the warden. The big bloated queen was his wife, and all the rest of the ants were prisoners, except for the big dumb ones with large jaws, which were cops. I began reciting their names when one of the guards hit me with a baton. Gosh, that hurt!

I remonstrated with them for being such spoilsports and not having a better sense of humor. They handcuffed me and took me to the warden. I offered to let them handcuff each of my prisoner ants, but they refused. The warden accused me of violating prison sanctity and being insubordinate. I told him he wasn't my boss that I had been married, but I got fired when I went to prison. He locked me in the hole for ten days. When I was free from the hole, I found out all my little prisoners had escaped. I hope they stung a whole bunch of people first. (Smile)

Finally after thirty-six months, D-day occurred. The parole board had a hearing. Two big cops came to the furniture shop, handcuffed me, and took me to meet the parole board. When it was my turn, I went in and met the big five from Burlingame, California. The spokesperson let me sit down, and then informed me they were taping everything I said and it could be used against me. They told me about the eleven-point matrix that determines your eligibility to go free. It was based on employment, education, previous arrest record, social standing previous to your arrest, recommendations of others, and your record of behavior while incarcerated. I got ten out of eleven points. They bade me to leave the room. I came back and they denied me parole. They asked me how I felt about their denial. I told them "real good, I am totally institutionalized. I love it here; I never want to be a free man again. Three hots and a cot are all I live for." A week later they cut me loose. I guess they thought I was crazy. That made me a good candidate for re-entering mainstream society.

The warden wanted some face time with me. I was escorted into the Sanctum Praetorium by the usual two big burly cops. They wanted to know where I wanted to parole to? I told them Seattle, Washington. They asked the usual questions. Did I have family there? "No." Did I know anyone there? "No". Did I have roots in the community there? "No." Did I know anyone there? No. I explained I had a dream telling me to go there. They were dumb struck. They told me to go back to work and they would let me know the outcome.

The parole board asked me a telling question; what were my impressions of prison. Big mistake, they should have never asked me that. I responded, "The court procedure reminded me that the mill of the Gods grinds slowly, but exceedingly fine. Prison reminded me of Dante's Inferno'; on the entrance post to Hell were inscribed the words "Abandon All Hope Ye Who Enter Herein," and on the exit portal "And This Too Will One Day Pass Away." They didn't ask me any more questions. I got to go to Seattle. I thought I was leaving the big sewer pipe, the cesspool of existence. I didn't care how they ejaculated or regurgitated me back into the real world. Little did I know that the mean streets of Seattle had its share of desperados running free and looking for someone to prey upon.

The Feds haberdashery is somewhat limited in fashionable attire, and at two hundred eighty six pounds I wasn't going to get single needle stitching and a Saville row suit. But I did receive green polyester pants, a lime green shirt, cardboard-soled shoes, one pair of shorts, two socks and a bus ticket. They cashed out my credits at the commissary, and funny thing, there was only enough to buy me a bus ticket to Seattle. I didn't stick around to argue. I took a Tylenol for my headache and jumped on Greyhound. The old loping dog looked mighty good right then. It's too bad they didn't stamp prisoner on my forehead, because everybody I talked to, seemed to know anyway. It must have been those swell spare no expense clothes they gifted me with. (Smile)

FREEDOM

I arrived in Seattle on July 2, 1981 at 1:00 p.m. and it was ninety-two degrees. I called the Bishop Lewis half way house. The Dragon Lady answered. She informed me I was late and I better get my fat ass up there as soon as possible, or she would violate me. I didn't know if she meant she would violate me personally or not, but from the tone of her voice, I bet she could do it. I pointed out that I couldn't arrive there before the bus did. I don't think that helped my case.

Seattle is built like Rome. I know I climbed at least seven hills getting to Eighth and Cherry. When I arrived there, they didn't leave the light on like Tom Bowdin always promised, just pale looking guys and Brunhilda. I swear, Louise looked like I imagined the harpies, or one of the four furies of the Valkyries would look. She made me feel about as welcome as my ex-mother-in-law used to make me feel whenever I visited the dairy farm in Idaho for soirees and social occasions, but I was used to being the bastard son at the family reunion.

Louise was violating a guy, and the cops were on their way to pick him up for being drunk and trying to drive off in his truck. She flipped me to the new guy she was training. He was about five feet ten inches tall and about one hundred fifty pounds, in a pair of docker pants, a white shirt and a blue velvet coat. I couldn't believe my eyes. The guy hadn't even broken a sweat and it was hot. I didn't know he had just returned from India, and compared to that place, he probably thought it was a cool mid-morning breeze. He invited me inside. I was wary, because he invited me instead of ordering me inside. He explained the rules, which were pretty simple. "Do what you are told to do, or you get to finish the rest of your sentence back behind walls. You need to report to a parole officer right away and get a job as soon as possible." I understood all that. It was crystal clear. I wasn't out of prison yet! I settled in, ate a meal, and watched T. V without any bars in front of it surrounded by convicts yelling. I showered, and went to bed in a room all by myself. I was King of the World.

PAROLE OFFICERS

I reported to the courthouse the next day. I met my assigned parole officer. What a trip down memory lane that was. It went something like this…"Hi, my name is Dave. I'm your new master, you will do whatever I say or I will screw you so bad you will wish to God you were back in prison. I can drop in on you, violate you, or do anything to you I want. I don't trust anybody. I don't like anybody. I don't have any friends. My family is marginal at best and if I see you anywhere near my neighborhood where I live, even if by accident I will shoot you dead! Any questions?"

I could only think of one, "Dave, why did you sugar coat it like that? You shouldn't hold back so much. Why didn't you speak more frankly and act more forthright with me?" He was still cursing when I left. I learned in prison, truly dangerous people don't threaten you up front.

With Dave I knew which way the wind was blowing, only one direction, from him to me.

I sent out seventy-two resumes. I had them printed at Sudden Printing. That became my de-facto office. I arranged nineteen interviews. I eliminated all but six of them. I'll tell you a carefully guarded secret. Very few people, be they men or women, know how to interview a potential employee properly. I usually blew them out of their shoes when we got down to the part of the interview where they tell you, "You are hired, and do you have any questions?"

I only had one…"I just got out of Federal prison for mail and wire fraud conspiracy, would that prevent me from getting the job? "When asked to elucidate further, I would explain, "I am eager to go to work for you. I have been locked down for three years. But, I don't like surprises and I have to assume you don't either. One day, somebody, probably my parole officer, will drop a dime on me and make an anonymous phone call, informing you I had been in prison. If you are faint hearted, I would rather know it now, than work my heart out for you and do an outstanding job, and six months from now, you call me in and tell me we have to talk because there is something significant that I didn't disclose to you initially. I eliminated all but six potential employers. I think I did real well. (Smile)

NEW JOB

I went to work selling illuminated signs for National Sign Company. There were two brothers that owned the company. It was the oldest and the best sign company in Seattle, but it was a union shop. I knew nothing about the sign wars that had taken place in Seattle fifteen years previously. I had just parachuted into town. All that meant to me was we had to charge more than the little independent shops.

The two brothers were Hungarian Catholics. They were devout. I didn't care; I had survived the nuns at the orphanage. Tony, the quiet one and the president of the company looked and talked like Robert De Niro. He could have been his double. He talked softly, but firmly. George was the muscle. He made dreams come true. He got the job done no matter what. They hired me with one caveat. They wanted to test drive me awhile on straight commission and see if I was the real deal, or if I was blowing smoke up their pants. They called my parole officer and got a heads up on me.

Dave, my parole officer, called me in and read me the riot act for telling them I was in prison. I thought it was kinda funny. Now I was the bad guy for telling the truth. What a world! Thirty days later they put me on salary plus commission. The brothers called me in and did the old congratulatory speech, and the you are getting a raise speech. I thanked them and asked, "What's the real reason you're giving me the golden apples of the sun and maybe your daughters hand in marriage?"

They didn't think that was very funny, but Tony dropped his guard and said "It's cheaper to have you on the payroll and pay you commission later, than pay it all up front." I thought that was very sensible of them.

National Sign Company has all the sign business at SeaTac International Airport. They still do. I worked for them for three years and I can tell you quite honestly they treated me better than anyone ever had in my whole life. They opened up the world to me and I made a ton of money with them. I heard they made a few bucks themselves. I left my mark all over Seattle. I even got to date beautiful topless dancers because I sold signs to the places where they worked.

RUNAWAYS

Because I got a job right away i.e. three weeks from the time I hit the half way house, I received special privileges. I could go out at night with a midnight curfew. I tried to catch up on all the movies I missed while I was behind walls. I could ride the free bus downtown and see a flick and stroll the waterfront. It felt great to be a semi-free man again. My parole officer trifled with me occasionally, but I wasn't hiding anything, so I didn't care.

While I was in the half way house I met a thirteen-year-old girl living in the bus station doorway. She offered to date me. After I explained I didn't date kids, cripples, or vulnerable people, I asked her when she ate last? She couldn't remember. I made her go into the bus station and eat Greyhound food. I told her it wouldn't kill her. It may taste like it's killing you, or like it's been dead itself for a while, but I eat it, and look how fabulous I look. She busted out laughing.

Her name was Susan. Her dad started molesting her when she was nine years old. Then he invited the neighbors to join the party in molesting his daughter. Her thirteen-year-old sister had already been pregnant with his child and had an abortion, so she took to the streets. She had some stories to tell. On the street, young kids like her are known as "Chicken Meat". You don't want to know the rest…We became friends. We still are. Even though she had three kids by three different men, none of them mine, I might add. She is married now, and is trying to live the American dream in Oregon. She had to leave the mean streets of Seattle. My wife and I went to her wedding last year. She is doing better.

I was the phone man at Bishop Lewis' half way house. The phone would ring and no one else would answer it. So by default, I would answer it. The calls became familiar. Some were real chilling and not fun to deliver. "Tell Kurt that his girlfriend has overdosed and he needs to come and get her!" "Sidney, that druggist you shot ain't gonna make it; you need to get out of there right away." "Tell Leonard I'm at the hospital; someone beat me up." Etc. But by far, the worst calls were the crying women and children who wanted to talk to the men who had wronged them.

When the men wouldn't talk to them, it was truly heart wrenching. But I couldn't fix the whole world; I was only the phone man.

My old friend, the psychiatrist, that I worked for when I was incarcerated at McNeil Island Penitentiary called me at the half way house. She told me that she decided to help a guy get out of Lompoc and move him into her big house in Poulsbo, Washington. I knew without asking that he must be a bank robber and he would give her those little spankings on her bare bottom that she liked so well. I suddenly understood the saying "different strokes for different folks". I guess it's okay when it's therapeutic in nature, and prescribed by an M.D. She wanted me to board the ferryboat and ride to Bremerton. She bequested me to be her personal slave and help her get her house ready so Ken and Donna could get married in her forty-four hundred square foot cottage. Shades of Leona Helmsley. I agreed to do it. Who could refuse such a generous offer?

Actually, I jest! Barbara was a brilliant conversationalist. She graduated first in her class at the Sorbonne. Her French was impeccable and she was delightful to be around. I didn't mind cleaning gutters, filling the coal bin, landscaping the yard, planting flowers, and fixing her cars. I got to swim in her lagoon on her private beach, gather cherry clams and black-lipped oysters, and fish for halibut. I could cook anything she liked in her fully equipped kitchen and share it with her. I just had to be careful that she didn't drink too much wine and make me miss my boat back to the world I lived in.

She gave me her 1964 Volvo station wagon that had deferred maintenance on it. The deal was, I got to drive the car until it was completely fixed, or she asked for it back. Since fixing all its problems would be tantamount to the twelve labors of Hercules, discovering fire, and inventing the wheel, I knew I would get to keep the car for a while.

She lived by Bangor Nuclear Submarine Base. I was interested in the Trident Missile Base there because they were trying to teach porpoises with strapped explosives and charge assigned targets, blowing up the enemy and themselves upon command. Unfortunately, porpoises are smarter than people. They don't use words to communicate with each other. They use three-dimensional images that they transmit with ultra high frequency sound waves to each other. Since sound travels six times faster in water than through the air, the porpoises got the picture very quickly. After a few were blown to smithereens, they refused to obey their captor's commands when it required self-destruction.

Too bad the United States Navy didn't recruit Palestinian porpoises. They might have been willing to see the program through to its conclusion. I was intrigued that they needed something dumber to do their underwater dirty work. Sea Lions turned out to be ideal. I noticed they succeeded for a few fish and some sweet talk to get them to self-destruct for the Navy Seal of Approval. Even as I write these lines they are currently employed in the Iraq attack.

Well, Ken and Donna moved in with Barbara. They arrived in a converted school bus. All their belongings were aboard. It was adorned with graffiti. It was like something out of the nineteen sixties period. It should have been called the hemp mobile, because clouds of sweet acrid smoke filtered out from its windows night and day. I attended the wedding ceremony. Barbara spent twenty thousand dollars getting her place ready for the occasion. It was written off as capital improvement expenditures. I'm not sure if the bride and groom heard the ceremony, or their mumbled responses, but it was the best trip they had ever taken to date.

They later took LSD and maybe some I.B.M. because a week later, they took a business trip. They held up a Hood Canal Bank and they both went away for ten years, courtesy of the United States Government.

CHANGES

I got out of the half way house early. Jim Kelly, the Catholic priest, who ran Bishop Lewis' halfway house, committed suicide. It seems he fathered a child. I guess the term Father is intended to be used metaphorically not literally. Too bad he couldn't have outlived the stigma until now. The Catholic Church recently reported thirty one percent of all nuns are abused. My convict experience makes me think they probably were nuns that disguised themselves as alter boys to get abused. I actually miss Father Kelly. He was forthright and honest with me. In the short time I spent under his aegis, he treated me fairly. The one rule I learned in Federal Prison that is sacrosanct and kept inviolate is the rule that no matter what happens, felons don't ever cry. It is chiseled into the stone of my heart.

I moved to an apartment in Edmonds, Washington, sixteen one-bedroom hovels built during the Seattle Worlds Fair as motel rooms. I affectionately called mine the black hole of Calcutta. It goes without saying; I didn't spend very much time there. It was owned by a Filipino couple that kept having mysterious fires. Since I didn't own a lot of valuables, I didn't care that they had three fires in three years. The insurance companies gave them enough money to build the Taj Mahal. They sold their travel agency and returned to the Philippines.

While I was selling signs, I met some very interesting players. One of them, Gary Tripp, seemed like a renaissance man to me. He owned the Tripp building up on Broadway. Broadway is on Capital Hill, a major promontory in Seattle. Seattle has lots of hills like San Francisco. Locals call it Pill Hill because we have seven major hospitals on the hill. Gary flew his own twin-engine plane, and had a black belt in karate, owned his own company, dated haute coutre models, and was a restaurant owner of some merit. He co-owned a restaurant and belonged to the café crowd that went nightclubbing every night.

Imagine my surprise when Robin, a beautiful model that modeled for Nordstrom, called me hysterical, crying and totally incomprehensible "Gary is trying to kill me." She blubbered.

"Impossible!" I replied "or you would be dead! Why would he do that? You're his main squeeze." She wouldn't tell me on the phone so I met her up town. She wanted to move in with me and have me protect her. Then she told me Gary offered twenty five thousand dollars for her dead or alive. I checked around and found out she was telling the truth.

I explained to her I never write checks with my mind that my body can't cash, but Bobby Lott is an ex-green Beret. He is a friend and she would be completely safe with him. Nobody gets past Bobby. They used to drop him into the jungle in Viet-Nam and his orders were to make sure that no one was left alive in the perimeter when they went in, that could impair their mission. He never failed in his assignments.

But, it begs the question; "Why does Gary want you dead?"

Her explanation was a definite eye opener. "Gary flew an eleven year old girl from Mexico into Seattle. He had her confined in a loft he owns. He has been using her for his personal sexual gratification. He had a video of them dancing on the bed with butt plugs in, etc." The rest is too gruesome to tell.

"Where is the child now?" I asked. I wanted to recover her and undo her trauma.

"She is gone." Robin said. "I took his tape while he flew back to Mexico, but he found out I had the tape."

I had Robin give me the tape. I delivered her safely to Bobby. The cops got the tape! Gary is doing fifteen years in Walla-Walla. I had to move fast because I knew once Bobby found out what Gary did he would whack him in a Seattle second.

Bobby now lives in Hong Kong with a beautiful Chinese lady, a woman of some considerable means. She wanted a white boy friend, especially one, with the fore part of one finger missing. In the Orient it is a sign of the Triad society. Robin still models and I see her pictures in the paper every once in awhile. Truth truly is stranger than fiction.

STREET LIFE

Seattle has a lot of homeless people and vagrants. There is a difference. The climate here is pretty mild. It doesn't get too cold in the wintertime, and there are food banks and churches that will spare you a few crumbs, or throw you a bone, if you really need one. Because I was single and the word got out down at the bus station at Eighth and Stewart that I would help, I soon got busy night and day. The phone would ring all hours of the night. During the day, I had an answering machine that fielded the calls. All I had to do was screen them and answer them in descending order of priority.

I clocked in one afternoon around five p.m. I was home early because I hadn't sold a damn thing. It was hot and I had a migraine. The fact that I had to wear a necktie that day had just added fuel to the fire. The call that lit up my personal switchboard was from a street girl I knew, Tina Ziggenfuse, a heroin addict. She had burned her baby's belly with a lit cigarette in a public restaurant in West Seattle because it was crying too much. I knew Philippe the father of the baby, and I knew he wasn't there. He would have hospitalized her for that. He really loved Roger; he was his little pride and joy.

I had tried to buy Roger from Tina so I could get him into a good home, but she wouldn't sell him because he was her meal ticket. It wasn't that I needed a kid. I could buy one up on Broadway for twelve hundred dollars anytime. You don't get to choose the sex, or nationality, but people buying babies generally don't care about that anyway. In Seattle, a woman can lose a kid to the State, then get it back in thirty days. All she has to do is say, "I've been clean and sober for thirty days," and DSHS sends the kid home with the birth mother.

Tina had five kids by five different guys. She lost them all to the State from time to time, but she always got them back for Christmas, so she could play Santa Claus, give them presents, visit her folks, turn some tricks, and get loaded again. If I knew of a poster child for Sterilization, she was it.

I knew I needed to beat feet over to West Seattle right away. Where were the other kids if she only had Roger at lunch with her? Most heroin addicts are not dangerous when they are on a nod. All they want to do is be left alone and nod out. It's when they wake up and need a fix and don't have one that they get dangerous. The word on the street is "You can ride the dragon, but you can't ever let go." I knew where Tina crashed. When I parked the car and started up the stairs, I could hear Vanessa and Tiffany crying.

I tried to remember what they taught me about opening locks with a credit card in Crime College, but the door had a deadbolt. I went downstairs and got the manager. He was reluctant to leave his beer and "The Price is Right" on T.V. When I explained that I was going to hold him as an accessory before the fact and after the fact he came alive. He asked me if I was a cop. I was still wearing a suit, the White Mans business uniform, so I told him, "more or less." It worked! I got the kids and took them to DSHS. Suddenly, I didn't feel so bad about not selling any signs that day. But I knew tomorrow was another day.

OLD ACQUAINTENCES

I met Butch inside prison. He was riding a murder beef. When you own a barbershop and you are cutting a guy's hair, no matter how mad you are at him, you shouldn't cut his throat with a straight razor. I pointed that out to Butch while we were both inside. I explained, "It was bad business for three reasons. One, the guy hadn't asked for a shave. Two, he forgot to cut the guys hair. And three, he didn't get paid for his services." He thanked me for sharing and proceeded to cut my hair. I wasn't worried; Butch needed me. He lost his appeal and needed a writ to get out. I could help him. He wouldn't kill me until after I wrote his writ for him. I knew Butch paid the rent on an apartment down on Mercer Street by the Seattle Center where the Space Needle was. I knew some other people that stayed there. Butch told me so. When I got out of the halfway house I wandered down there one day.

I rang the buzzer, used Butch's name, and got buzzed into the building. I went to apartment #105. The door was open and inside was a tall, lanky, older guy. He told me his name was Les. I figured that was his street name.

On the street everyone has a moniker i.e. Parking meter Bill, he robs parking meters. Ding Dong, she is mentally challenged. Tobey two fingers, he dips wallets. He dipped the wrong guy. The guy cut off the fingers he didn't need with pruning clippers. Peeler, he peels safes. There are only three ways to open a locked safe without the proper combination, peeling is one of them. But Les, it turned out, was this guy's real name. I came to tell him he had to pay the rent on the apartment from now on. Butch had died inside the prison of a massive coronary. Les nodded agreement and thanked me for letting him know the status quo.

There were two little bubble gum girls with Les. They were upset that they had to hit the bricks again. Les consoled them. He was a longshoreman on the docks at night and played the ponies during the days. He even had a horse of his own. He lived at Emerald Downs when he wasn't working the docks. I noticed his eyes were clear as crystal, cobalt blue. He didn't do drugs. I was impressed, but I knew he was an alky. Alcoholics have a look and pallor all their own.

I knew a guy on the docks; a foreman named Mike Stages. Les said he knew him, too. I knew Mike's old lady worked for Seattle First National Bank. I also knew he partied with run away underage girls, chicken meat, because I saw his Cadillac Seville at the Pike Street Market looking for girls in the early mornings. I didn't like the guy. Les didn't either. He hated him because he broke into the cargo containers and robbed them I hated him because he hurt a couple of the girls, and I had to take them to Harbor View Hospital to get them repaired. The girls got him back though. They stole his wife's jewelry and left some thong panties in her bed. They fenced the jewelry at Ben Bridges jewelry store at Northgate.

Mike's wife divorced him. What goes around comes around. (Smile)

BINGO

Once I got caught up on all the old movies I missed while I was down for the count, I found a new way to divert myself. I started going to Chinatown at night. I was learning Kung Fu and making new friends, and the food was the best I had ever eaten. After all I was in the very place Bruce Lee was established as an institution. I met some high-ranking members of the Chinese Tong. They were very courteous and polite to me. They extended invitations to attend social events and to meet men of respect. But no matter how long you may know or consort with Orientals, theirs is a closed society. As an occidental you will never really know them intimately. As one of them told me with a smile, "We Chinese have been conquered by everybody. But where are our conquerors now? We have outlived them all." His point being, even Bruce Lee died eventually, but the Chinese people live on as a group. The focus is not upon the individual, but the group.

The Chinese Tong is referred to as a Benevolent Fraternal Order, or Society. It has existed for thousands of years. If you violate or wrong them, they extinguish all your living relatives for four generations. But if you benefit them, they never forget it.

I was invited to a Chinese wedding. Inside I befriended a man named Cliff Stone. He owned *The Rainier Avenue Bingo Hall.* He was an ex-party whip in Olympia for the Democratic Party. Rainier Avenue is on the bad side of Seattle. It is a high crime corridor. Mostly minorities, Blacks, Asians, and Latinos frequent it.

Cliff donated eight hundred thousand dollars each year to the Democratic Party from the proceeds of his family owned Bingo operation. One rainy night two large men came into the bingo hall at closing time. They introduced themselves to Cliff and explained their purpose in coming was a change of plans. No more money was to be sent straight to Washington D.C.; there was new legislation that required scrutiny they didn't want. They explained the new plan and gave him deposit slips for a San Diego Bank. Cliff threw them out.

A few months later, two bigger meaner men came into the bingo hall at closing time. They pistol whipped Cliff and his two sons. They explained with some considerable intensity that this was not a voting matter. Cliff got to his gun and killed one of them; the other guy fled. The cops got the bad guy, but some one bailed him out. Now, here is the rub.

If you kill someone in Seattle and you are not a cop, you go see John Henry Brown, or Tony Savage. You pay their retainer. You will be arraigned but free on your own recognizance. You get to bail out until the trial. You do exactly what your council advises and you will never do a day behind bars. But Cliff got nervous and when he took the stand, he forgot the well-rehearsed script. Instead of "I was mortally afraid for my own life and perceived he was going to kill me, so I shot him in self defense." Cliff's scenario was, "The gun went off by accident." The jury didn't buy that; the gun went off by itself eight times.

He lost his retainer and lost his case. But, when I finished his writ he no longer had to do hard time. Audrey and the family could visit him and they stuck with him and shepherded him through the system.

Hence, when he got, out they invited me to their son's wedding to a marvelous Chinese girl born with a clubfoot, but the compassion of God and the heart of an Angel. She was wonderful. It was the best wedding I ever attended in my life, and I used to work on weekends for a caterer.

Because Cliff was a convicted felon, he and Audrey and the thirteen other members of his family had to give up the Bingo business. They moved to California and went to work for his son's construction company. Oh well "Alls well that ends well."

THE DRAGON

Herb Smith sold more heroin in Seattle then anyone in the great Northwest had ever done before. So when the Federal Government took him down, they did it so hard and fast, it made the fillings in his teeth ache. The public sees cocaine as a rich mans' harmless Bolivian marching powder. But heroin is perceived as the sweat of the devil. Anyone using it is personified as a demon incarnate. The feds sent Herb to Rahway, New Jersey, then to Marion, Ohio, two very bad places, complete lockdown and total scrutiny all the time. Herb did ten years hard time. Then he paroled to Seattle.

He got the Federal Government to buy him a six-bedroom house in a nice residential area. He started a program called Interaction Transition, I.T. for short. It was supposed to be a stepping-stone for men behind walls to gradually make their way back into mainstream society. Sometimes it worked.

I started going to their meetings every Wednesday night. Herb Smith fell because he broke the two cardinal rules of being a good heroin distributor. "Never get high on your own supply". Otherwise, you become your own best customer. Secondly, you must be totally ruthless. Kindness is perceived as weakness on the street.

I have been everybody's' designated driver for as long as I can remember. I've never done any drugs or alcohol. I perceive Indians don't have a good track record with these substances. I have watched too many people go down in flames to not be intimately familiar with their cause and effect.

I started going to I.T. out of boredom. There were sixty men and nineteen women attending. Everybody had a story and they loved to tell it, over, over and over again. The women either had a family member or paramour behind walls, or they had done time themselves. The men were just angry that their game had been interrupted.

Now, Herb had completely kicked the dragon. He didn't do heroin anymore. He got the Federal Government to buy the house and pay him to do a program with the bad guys. It worked for him! But nature and alcohol came rushing in. Nature abhors a vacuum, so it rushed in to fill the empty void.

CRIMINALS AND GRANDMAS

There was an extremely sensuous woman named Marnie that attended the meetings. With that group, it was like throwing gasoline on a raging bonfire. All the men went berserk trying to impress her with their I'm the toughest, sharpest guy that ever lived routine. She married Herb Smith.

I asked her "why?"

She said "Every man has a dick; it's what's in their wallet that makes a difference." It really took the bloom off the rose and dashed all my illusions about romantic love.

I met a seventy-two year old, highly educated, eighty-four pound grandma there. Her name was Francis Bartholemew. She had been a schoolteacher. She was frail looking, with porcelain skin, and silver blue hair. She just did not belong in that setting. Until I got to know her better, I almost thought I could smell cookies baking whenever I was around her. She was so delicate and refined; I waited a long time to hear her complete story. After I heard it, I got to know her and we became best friends. She was vegetarian mostly. She couldn't help doing McDonald's Chicken McNuggets or an occasional lamb chop. She did a little wine, and toked a little grass (but never around me) to go to sleep at night. But, she explained to me that they were perfectly natural substances that helped her relax, so she wouldn't eat meat. I took her everywhere she needed to go. She would call me to take her to her doctor's appointments. She had Parkinson's disease.

She was also a retired nurse and nanny. She raised a very rich mans family here in Seattle and tutored rich peoples children for supplemental income. Every Christmas we exchanged books for presents to each other. I even got her interested in visiting the bad girls at Purdy, the women's prison, with myself, and some other people every Tuesday night. She really made us tow the line. There was no radio playing allowed in my car. She was the only one allowed to sit up front except for the driver. She had a snack going, and a snack on the way home. She may have looked frail, but she definitely wasn't. She was like bamboo. Let me tell you her story.

Francis was born in Canada. She came to Seattle as a college graduate because America paid more money for schoolteachers and nurses. She saved her money, was very frugal, and ended up buying a coop apartment up on Denny Street. As her Parkinson's disease progressed her physical strength diminished, although I doubt if she was ever very robust.

A very nice young man named Steven started helping her open her door because the key stuck frequently. He lived across the hall from Francis and worked at Goodyear tire store in downtown Seattle. Soon they started eating together each night, her place or his.

Then she introduced him to what I called a woo-woo church. *The Eternal Temple of Truth and Light.* They had seven women that ran and owned it. They did séances and conjured spirit visitations. They also owned a gaming license and a bingo parlor. Boy, did they ever make money. It was unbelievable how well they did.

Two years later Francis wanted to have sex with Steven. He was much younger than her. He decided to come clean with her. It was mind numbing what he told her. "Francis, I'm an escaped prisoner from Walpole Prison in the State of Massachusetts. I murdered a man when I was seventeen years old. Two friends and I held up a convenience store. We took beer and tried to take the money. The clerk wouldn't give it to us willingly. We had been drinking. I took a claw hammer and beat his brains out with it. We took the register and the beer. We busted the register open in the woods. We got sixty-eight dollars. If only the clerk had given us the cash, none of that would have happened. The men in prison just used me and passed me around to each other. I couldn't take it any longer. I pretended to be sick and I escaped from the hospital, changed my identity, and moved here."

Francis never missed a beat. "It's you and me honey! We will run away together and they will never find us." They pooled their money. Francis sold her antiques and her apartment, and they went on the lam together.

Two years later in Albuquerque, New Mexico the F.B.I. arrested them both living together in a motor home. Francis had a nursing job and Steven worked for Kelly Tires. The F.B.I. told Francis "Your I.D. is so good that if I didn't know who you were, I would believe your cover story." Well, the rest is history. They cut Francis loose for time served. Nobody wanted to prosecute everybody's grandma. You couldn't help thinking of warm chocolate chip cookies fresh out of the oven every time you saw her. They took Steven back to prison, where unfortunately, he died behind prison walls. Francis died a few years later after waiting patiently for him to flatten out his sentence. But you know, I bet, if they were to drive away into the sunset today with the music playing softly in the background, Hollywood would find some way to make a blockbuster movie of the whole episode. I know this time I'd buy a ticket for sure just to see it happen.

THE HOT LINCOLN

Malashi Johnson has the Lincoln used in the Hart to Hart television show. He has it hidden in a garage up on Capitol hill off an alley I know. Malashi uses it to pick up young girls that hang out up on Broadway. He turns them onto drugs, and then turns them out.

He used the car to rob a UPS truck a few Easters ago. He runs most of the drugs in the Rainer Valley. He stole the car from Bank of America. He keeps changing the plates to keep from getting caught. He is a two-bit player. On the street they are known as popcorn pimps. I don't have any use for the dude because he used one of his own people to hurt a respectable guy that runs a janitorial business.

Tom gave him a job and vouched for him to get a credit profile. Tom had worked as a shoeshine boy in Chicago. He also worked as railroad conductor, waiter, busboy, and other menial jobs to get ahead. He saved his money, bought a business, got married and raised a family. Tom is now sick and in a convalescent home.

Malashi perceives he got over on the system, his friend, and everybody. I wait patiently for the God of Vengeance to right the wrong. But sometimes you have to wait a long time.

EVIL

Robbie was a black man with a black heart, if he had one at all. He was one of the truly evil men I met while I was in prison. In the early days of Western Union, the American Indians pulled down the "talking wires" because they knew the white man communicated with them. They knew that the white man could send news faster than a smoke signal or a pony could run. Inside the prison, they have the grapevine. Marvin Gaye sang "he heard it from the grapevine: After his dad killed him with a 30-30 rifle some folks said, "he heard if from the carbine."

Inside, everyone has a nickname or jacket. Usually it is related to their crime, or some facet of their personality. Mine was the professor, because I worked in the prison library. I read a lot and I had a small amount of formal education. Robbie's handle was Mamba, or Black Death. He gloried in it. On the outside, he was a crack dealer in Tacoma. He was totally ruthless. Some cruelty is expected because of circumstances, but unnecessary cruelty is deplored and considered overkill even in prison. Robbie stabbed a guy in the throat with a sharpened toothbrush because he got the last piece of pie at dinner. He cut a faggot's throat with a pocket comb just because the guy was queer. Now I never had a lot of use for the sugar pants boys, but usually they were not much of a threat to anyone except to themselves and each other.

For instance, I had a pet cat with broken legs I called Stubby. A demented Hawaiian inmate took him up to the tenth tier and threw him off. He let the cat fall one hundred feet onto the concrete floor to see if cats always land on their feet. It broke Stubby's legs and his broken body was picked up by one of the murderers on the ground floor and they threw his body into the bushes outside because nobody expected him to live. Stubby must have had eight lives left because I found him living under the steps to the dining hall a week later. I fed him something and from then on he was my cat. He waited for me patiently after every meal. Before long, lots of guys started saving morsels of food for me to feed Stubby. It was sort of comical to see what the Mexicans called my low rider cat trundling along behind me whenever I walked the yard. It was nice to have someone care about me, even though he was just a cat.

Later somebody slipped some ground glass into the crazy Hawaiian dude's food. He had to say Aloha to the boys in the big house and they sent him to Springfield prison for surgical throat repairs. The other Hawaiians said he was pu-pule, which means totally crazy in any language you choose to use, but I digress...

We had a mean boat captain named McCormack. He liked to kill runaway inmates. He had killed six of them in the fifteen years he had been on the island. Everyone knew the water was eight hundred feet deep. It was cold and at forty-nine degrees you couldn't last very long.

The currents were swift and strong, and even if you weren't missed for thirty minutes or so, you would eventually wind up on driftwood Annie's Beach.

She would bring you in and give you hot soup or coffee, call the cops and you would be back in custody within a few hours, usually with additional time to serve. Mack always volunteered to hunt the dirty dogs down and shoot them dead, even when the other cops told him to take it easy. He was uncanny at predicting exactly what the escapee would do, and exactly which way they would run. He shot a couple of the would be escapees off the fence with an old favorite 30-30 rifle he kept on the boat.

Lots of guys had to take turns working on the boat. It was the only way on and off the island. My turn came up, so I had to shift gears and priorities for a while. Since I had worked as a fisherman in Alaska for three summers to put myself through college, it was kind of pleasant to be back on the water. I kept getting written up for talking to the officer's wives and children and helping them on and off the boat when the weather was rough and the boat pitched and heaved a lot.   Inmates weren't supposed to fraternize with anyone that wasn't incarcerated. I thought it was stupid to watch some officer's wife burdened with little children and groceries struggle to board and unboard the boat without helping them, so I did what I thought was necessary.

One day during a storm, Mack ordered me to jump to the dock and tie off the boat while we were still pitching and heaving and moving forward too fast. He was in a particularly foul mood, so when I asked him to go around again or back up the boat, he refused with considerable vehemence. He let out a string of particularly colorful curses and said, "I'm ordering you to do it. I don't give a damn how dangerous it is."

I lifted his 30-30 off the hook on the cabin wall and told him, "I presume this is loaded. Well guess what, elephants don't jump, rhinos don't jump, and at two hundred eighty six pounds, I don't jump. Now, if you want to fight about it, make your move. I don't trust you to not have an accident and shoot me in the back, so I'm throwing your gun overboard and you can come back and get it later. "I tossed the gun overboard.

He ordered me out on deck while he radioed for back up to meet us back on the prison side of the island. They took me to the hole for insubordination.

Like I told them, "I've been in solitary before, it ain't nuthin." When I hit the hole and they locked me down, a big cop named Robinson from Mississippi that I helped form a corporation came to see me. He asked me what happened; when I told him, he thought it was funny. He told me Mack never mentioned anything about the gun because it would have gone in his file that he lost control of his weapon.

Well, the bad part of this story is while I languished in the hole, they hired Robbie to work the boats. As soon as he spotted the thirteen-year-old autistic deaf white girl, he laid his plan to get her. She rode the boat daily to attend a special school on the mainland in Tacoma. One day she got off the boat just as Robbie ended his shift. He followed her up the hill. When no one could see him, he pulled her into the bushes. He brutally raped her and traumatized her so badly that she wasn't found for hours. She was still huddled in the bushes curled in the pre-natal position with her pants, and underwear around her ankles. She couldn't talk, only gasp, cry and moan. She was hospitalized for days. The only way they could get her to sleep at all was with the light on, a nurse in the room, and a drip with drugs going into her veins. Her dad, the cop, let the prison grape vine know that whoever did this to his daughter was a dead man walking. He offered five thousand dollars cash to anyone that would kill the perpetrator, or five thousand dollars to anyone that would finger him so he could kill the perpetrator himself. The warden found out and had to transfer the entire family. Eventually, word leaked back to him about the game that was afoot, as Sherlock Holmes would have said.

Well the grapevine was humming, but nobody confessed. A sudden pall fell over the prison and everything went into slow motion. Everyone was talking, but nobody was saying anything that mattered. A year later the truth came out, as it always does eventually.

Fat Paul ran the prison laundry and most of the black population on the island. He weighed in at over four hundred fifty pounds, but he moved with dignity and grace. No one ever disputed his authority. Paul and I played handball doubles against all challengers. We played for Pepsi Cola because they only had Coca Cola in the commissary and Pepsi had to be brought in by special order. That made it precious stuff. We could get five dollars a can easy for it. We had never been beaten, and as the reigning prison champions we weren't shy about letting the general population know that if they didn't mind losing money, we were available for a quick pick-up game anytime. I used to tell Paul he reminded me of a cross between Fat Albert, Jackie Gleason, and Barishnoikov. He had the moves of a dancer.

The only reason Paul was in prison was he did everything bigger than life. He used to deliver some very high priced whores anywhere in Portland to the nicest hotels in a beautiful yellow Rolls Royce Cornishe. He was well known by the police, the doormen, and the concierges of all the major hotels. He never threatened or abused his girls. He treated them well and they could leave the trade anytime they wanted to do so.

He owned a nice restaurant, an upscale pool hall, a Laundromat, and other properties. However, Portland got a new Jewish Governor who later got himself kicked upstairs to Washington D.C. and became the commissioner of transportation and highways. In the shuffle he decided to make a name for himself by taking down high profile cases. Neil took down Paul, and Paul was doing his time. When Paul came to me with a big frown on his face, I knew something bad had happened. He asked to call a favor from me. In my usual reserved way I said, "It depends."

He said, "I want you to pull a nigger's jacket for me."

I asked "Who?" since he had never asked me for such a favor before.

"Robbie's," He answered.

"Why" I asked.

Paul said "He is bragging that he raped that little white girl a year ago; I'm cutting that boy loose. I want everyone to know he is dead. That nigger doesn't have my protection; he is on his own. He stands for everything I hate in black people and in anyone else that lives his way."

Well, I did the favor and it was worse than either of us had imagined. Robbie got his sister hooked on crack cocaine, and then he turned her out, and made her work the Tacoma bus station. He had killed his mother with a kitchen knife, and then had sex with her dead body for three weeks before the cops finally found and apprehended him in the house with the dead body. He was a sick and disgusting son-of-a-bitch in our book. Paul put out the word that he was a dead man walking. He never caught wind of it until someone helped him learn to fly seventy feet above the cement floor. He screamed all the way down.

Convicts have a code of justice that is unique to them. They call it doing the birdie. Some rated his diving score as very low by Olympic standards. I noticed in particular that he didn't fare as well as Stubby my little low rider cat did. I don't know anyone that shed a tear for him, but I heard some of the men lit a candle in the prison chapel for the little white girl.

BULLETS AND DONUTS

Gunther Manhalt ran the donut shop downtown at First and Pike Street. He sold a lot more than just donuts. If you needed a run away kid to be your bed partner at night, a nice watch or other piece of expensive jewelry, and you didn't want to pay full price, you went to Gunther. The kids liked him because he was open all night and if you wanted to hang out and get out of the rain or cold, Gunther was your man. Gunther took custom orders for people, too. If you needed a special kind of camera, a television, a stereo for your car, or home, Gunther could get it for you.

He had a chief lieutenant that kept everybody in line. His name was Wheels. He had his legs blown off by a claymore land mine in Viet Nam. He carried a 357 magnum on his chest, held in place by a leather thong. He wore his military clothes with patches, emblems and all his colors. Wheels patrolled the streets with great vigor and a nasty attitude. You didn't want to cross him or short him on a business deal. I saw him wheel into the Sunshine Inn one day at full speed. He rolled in, stabbed a guy and took him to the floor because the guy came up light on a drug delivery.

The Sunshine Inn was on Second and Pike. You could flop there for a few hours, meet tricks, a dealer, or a friend. But if you wanted the traditional soup and sandwich they served you had to listen to a sermon first. If you listened to the sermon you received the soup, the sandwich, a clean hypodermic needle so you wouldn't get hepatitis and a prophylactic if you wanted one. It was Seattle's battle plan to counter the drug epidemic, diseases of addicts and unwanted children.

Gunther would still be ensconced in the belly of the beast ruling his fiefdom if he hadn't sold a stolen gun picked up in a home invasion robbery. Gunther perceived that if Wheels filed the serial number off the gun, not even the F.B.I. could trace it. Someone bought the gun along with a dozen of Gunther's finest donuts. The dude used it to "off his old lady" and the rest is history.

The not so happily married man decided to do the job himself. He thought if he threw the gun into Elliott Bay, no one would ever find it. He was wrong! The insurance company smelled something fishy. They don't like paying claims, anyway. They stalled the chump. An amateur diver found the gun. He turned it over to the police who called in the F.B.I. The federal boys used acid to etch and retrieve the serial number. Eventually the trail of breadcrumbs led to the donut shop, which gave them Gunther. A few months after Gunther went away to Walla-Walla Penitentiary, Wheels was found tied to his wheelchair upside down in Elliott Bay.

The big money from California had come into town. Now you wouldn't recognize the guts of Seattle downtown. Condominiums dot the waterfront. The Temple of Venus is gone. Werner Rienhart would let you make a love offering to his Venusian love goddesses and then they would make a love offering back to you. One hour on television with Morey Safer ruined all that. He called it "thinly veiled prostitution." I thought that was harsh and prejudicial to label them so egregiously. However, I guess you couldn't argue in court that it out weighed its probative value. They say you know you are going to have a bad day when you wake up and find Morey Safer, Mike Wallace and a camera crew on your front steps ringing the doorbell.

The fishbowl is still downtown. You can slip into a booth, pop some quarters into a slot and watch lusty women undress and press parts of their body up against the glass partition in a provocative manner. You can fantasize anything you want as long as you have enough quarters to pay for it.

The arcade is gone, but the owner moved up the street and runs a private club with a marquee advertising "live nude girls inside now." I understand that for five dollars everyone can be

a member of his private club. That skirts the law
rather than the girls. I thought it imaginative that
he perceived live nude girls would attract more
revenue than advertising dead nude girls on stage
now.

POLITICAL CLOUT

Flashback:

I was in the hole again. The cops had stolen my Christmas presents and were taunting me daily. They owed me seventy-two dollars in back wages and sixteen dollars for stamps. I flew a kite to the prison chaplain. In lay-mans terms this means I sent a written request to the chaplain to make an inquiry in my behalf. When he asked about the aforementioned items, the warden flipped out and had me locked in the dungeon again. When you're in the white man's hell, this was a huge amount of money. On the outside this would be tantamount to a thousand dollars. When you consider I had worked three jobs at nine cents per hour trusting Mr. BOBO (the man) to pay me what I was due, I was incensed that I let them get into me so far.

Kindness is weakness, inside and outside of prison walls. I let my fingers do the walking. I dropped a dime on the warden. I ratted them off big time. I called the Washington Hot Line. I got Senator Orrin Hatch. He called the warden and threatened a Congressional Investigation and said things like, "When I get through tossing that place, you will be outside on the street with a cardboard sign saying I will work for food, job, or anything." I got this second hand from the warden in between shouted expletives, pejoratives, and vituperous scatological word impact.

It may be hearsay in the courts of law, but I got his drift. The next thing I knew I was paid in full. Nevertheless, catch twenty-two, I was back in the hole in what is known inside as a death cell. If you become too big a nuisance to the system, they lock you down with a guy riding a murder beef. They can only kill a murderer once; no matter how many people he kills. Murderers know this, so the death penalty doesn't act as an effective deterrent. Inside, a guy can earn extra privileges like more time in the yard, a second desert, or better food and clean clothing if he does a favor for the man. When they threw me in with a contract killer, I knew I had played them a little too close. I should have cut them some slack. Especially when they said, "You guys are both ex-Mormons; I hope you don't self-destruct," and laughed. It was a mean laugh, not friendly at all. I knew instantly what that meant. It was him or me.

CONTRACT KILLER

When they brought John Creech into my cellblock, I recognized him immediately; I had seen him featured on America's Most Wanted show on television. All the convicts watch that show. They hope they will be featured and gain some notoriety. I thought that was twisted logic, but I'm nobody, so my vote didn't count. I knew Creech was number one on the F.B.I.'s most wanted list; he had taken contracts and killed twenty-two men that they could prove and they suspected him of filling contracts they couldn't prove. They were taking him back to Boise, Idaho.

The three television shows all the inmates in the general population liked to watch the most were, America's Most Wanted, Women in Prison, and a daytime television show where the master of ceremonies yells "Come on down," because they always picked girls with big breasts that bounced when they ran. Now you know why I read most of the time and rarely watched television. Besides, the guys orchestrate which show the guard is supposed to turn to by screaming the loudest for the channel they wanted the most. It was pandemonium at best, let alone, straining to see it through the bars with guys yelling and talking.

When the U.S. Marshals and the required two big cops led in John Creech, quite a few guys recognized him. When they heard the guard's sobriquet to me, they knew something interesting was about to happen. I let Creech crash on the bottom bunk. He was alert, quiet, polite, and unassuming. All the real dangerous guys I met are that way. You can't survive if you pound your chest and yell that you're the meanest beast in the jungle. You'll scare someone too much; they will overestimate the threat to their person and take you out as an act of self-preservation.

At night when the prison shuts down for the day at ten p.m. and the furor of daily activity subsides and the beasts are locked in their individual cages, there is relative peace and quiet. Although, there are a few random voices yelling and fifty to sixty radios all playing at the same time, not necessarily on the same station. The two things that you first lose in prison, that you miss the most, are privacy and quiet.

AMERICAS MOST WANTED

After things settled down for the night, Creech wanted to talk. We were on our respective bunks. Creech asked me, "What are you in for?"

"Mail and Wire Fraud conspiracy," I told him.

He exclaimed "Oh, a white-collar criminal, huh? How much did they get you for?"

The darkness breeds familiarity like a campfire at night. Two hundred twenty eight million dollars," I answered.

He laughed, "You obviously didn't get the money, or you wouldn't be here."

I agreed. "How about you?" I asked. One of the rules of the road is you don't ask a man what he is charged with directly unless he opens the door first. He opened the door. So I walked through it.

"I'm a white collar criminal, too," he said. "I heard you used to be a Mormon."

I replied that I had been, but I had begged them for excommunication because I was embarrassing them to tears by being on the television, and in the Oregonian News Paper every day for 17 weeks. The Mormons were reluctant to excommunicate me, but eventually they acquiesced and capitulated upon my continual request for them to do so.

I asked John how he figured he was a white collar criminal if he killed people for a living.

His reply startled me. "I only killed people that deserved to die. I was just a businessman performing a much-needed service to a society that had no provision to provide for itself. I'm only going to be here one night, maybe two night's tops. Let me tell you my side of the story before they take me to Boise and kill me for killing people that were human garbage. I won't be here long enough to earn extra privileges, so I won't kill you in your sleep like the cops want me to do. I know why they put me in a kill cell with you.

"Whew, what a relief," I sighed, "now I only have to sleep with one eye open."

He laughed:

Here then, is the John Creech story spun for me one night in a solitary cell at McNeil Island penitentiary in the dark of night. Just a narrative, uninterrupted except for an occasional cough, or sneeze from surrounding cells where I knew other people were listening. Inside prison even the walls have ears. Somebody is always listening, and somewhere, somebody is watching too. Like I said earlier, the three things you first lose when you go to prison are your privacy, peace, and quiet. You don't get them back until you leave prison walls far behind.

John began his story: "I was raised a good Mormon boy from Horse Shoe Bend, Idaho. It's just a small town, a few miles from Boise. When I was a boy coming up, it was merely a bend on the Boise River, a few dirt scrabble farms, and ranches. We milked a few cows, had some chickens and a couple of horses. We went to the

Mormon Church in Boise. We had an old black and white T.V. and a battered old pick-up truck. I had a couple of brothers and sisters. I grew up going to "primary" as a youngster. I went to Mutual and joined the Boy Scouts. I even became an eagle scout, and earned my Duty to God award. I graduated from high school, joined the Marines and went to Viet Nam.

When I came back, I moved to Boise, and attended Boise State University. My second year I met a girl and we got married in the Mormon Temple. For two years I worked and studied. By the third year we had two kids and I took another job to make ends meet. We never had enough money. My night job was a janitorial job, cleaning offices in town and classrooms on campus. We were struggling, but we were as happy as we could be under those circumstances.

"I finished work one Sunday night and started for home after catching a bite to eat with my boss. By the time I got home it was around 4:30 A.M. When I arrived at my apartment and wheeled into the parking lot, I noted our front door was ajar. There was only one door, so I was seriously alarmed. When I went inside, I was not ready for the scene from hell that greeted me. Nobody could have withstood what I saw.

There on the bed was my naked wife trussed up with duct tape. Her ankles were taped together. Her wrists were taped in back of her. She was dead! She suffocated because of the duct tape over her mouth. Later, forensic studies found three men's sperm inside her. Three different men had taken turns raping her. My baby girl's body was thrown on the bed where they had taped her mouth shut and cut her throat ear to ear. She had bled out. My eight-month-old baby boy was stabbed repeatedly in the chest and stomach. I found him where one of the men had kicked his dead body under the bed. I died with them that night. Why us I wanted to know."

At first, the cops and everyone in town thought I did it. However, the cops found out I had an airtight alibi. They did more forensic studies, while I attended my family's funerals.

"The Mormons brought me food and looked after my needs. I quit going to church because it just embarrassed other people and they were at a loss for words, but so was I. After awhile the police quit taking my calls. They wouldn't return my calls and everything came to a standstill. The case wasn't closed, but it went into the cold case file and I was forgotten. My family was forgotten to everybody but me."

"I bought a gun, quit my job, and hired a private detective, in that order. I practiced with my pistol every day until I could drive a dime at thirty yards over and over again. It took a year, but my detective did his job and I found out who the three animals were that killed my family and stole my future from me. For some extra money, he even got me photographs and addresses."

"I didn't care if the cops caught me after I killed these three sick bastards; I just wanted to avenge my family's deaths. I didn't even use a silencer on the first guy. I walked over to his car while he was getting into it to go to work. He lived in Latoon, Pennsylvania. He still had one leg out of the car and was sitting down when I told him: I'm John Creech, you killed my family in Boise and I shot him once in the stomach. Everyone I talked to said it's the most painful place to be shot. When his eyes got big with recognition, I said: Here is a present from hell. I expect to see you there someday and I shot him between the eyes. I calmly walked away. I drove my rental car to the airport and flew away.

"The next guy worked construction in Los Angeles, California. I drove up to him at a stop sign, rolled my passenger window down, and motioned him to roll his drivers window down. I wanted to talk to him. He did and I said: I have a present from Boise for you. I drilled him in the temple. It was too easy. I used a high grade, custom made silencer this time."

"The next guy, I found tending bar in San Francisco. I went in and ordered a drink. I was in a suit. I looked like a businessman and he tried to chat me up and I let him. Where are you from he asked when he brought me my drink. I made sure I didn't touch anything, including my drink. Boise, Idaho, I said, have you ever been there? No I never have he exclaimed. Sure you have, you and two of your friends raped and killed my wife there. He froze like a deer caught in the headlights of a rushing car. I shot him between those two big filled with fear eyes of his. Even though it was 3:'00 P.M. in the afternoon and broad daylight, there weren't very many people in the bar room. The small caliber gun with a brand new silencer just made a spitting sound. He never made a peep; he just sat down hard behind the bar and slumped over. Once again, it was too easy. I went to my hotel. I watched the news, read the papers, went out for awhile and ate dinner. I wondered what to do next? All my enemies were dead! I walked the streets for awhile and realized that if I killed every strange freak I saw in San Francisco, I would run out of bullets before they ran out of freaks.

I moved to Portland, Oregon. It had the same small town feel as Boise. I heard from someone that an attorney in town was looking for a hit man for two hundred forty thousand dollars. I let someone check it out for me. It was for real. From that time until now, I never killed anyone else for free."

"I took one or two jobs a year and I got really good at it. I think of myself as a custom butcher, but I kill only vermin, human scum that have wronged others all their mis-begotten, miserable lives and deserved to die a hundred times over."

"I did the world a favor. I did what the world wanted done, but didn't have the guts or the legal permission to do. I make no excuses for myself. I am an un-repentant sinner and I know I will burn in hell for all eternity. But you know what, I did the work quickly, and cleanly without undue prolonged suffering. That's more than the

State is going to do to me. I would rather take a bullet than squirm around with my veins full of acid and paralyzed so I can't cry out."

I told him, "Maybe he could get his execution transferred to Utah, like Gary Gilmore had done. They still had death by firing squad in Utah. He could bite the bullet in Utah for sure."

Well, John Creech didn't get to die in Utah like he wanted to. Instead he was transported back to Idaho. He escaped once by having a gun smuggled into him while he was in prison on death row in Idaho. However, they apprehended him again in Seattle less than a year later down on Second and Cherry Street. A citizen recognized him from T.V. and called the cops. I still believe that you cannot out run the Television, or the massive exposure it gives.

He probably wouldn't have been happy in Utah anyway. I told him that I've heard the Mormons will let you pick the way you choose to die. You may even get to choose between a very stylish hood or wear a blindfold. But I doubt seriously if they would let you have a final cigarette. The Mormons don't want to let you die smoking, drinking coffee, tea or alcohol either. He almost died laughing. We both drifted off to sleep. I wasn't worried about him killing me because I am a very light sleeper.

MONEY

There is a saying on the street that when money talks, everyone listens. When five hundred million dollars came into town, everybody cleaned up their act. A new seventy six-story skyscraper was constructed by Martin Selig called the Columbia Tower. It eclipsed everything else on the skyline. Kemper Freeman, who humbly calls himself Mr. Bellevue, is attracting all the money from downtown Seattle to the East side. He and his financial backers are as busy as squirrels burying nuts in a hurricane. They have crafted a Brave New World.

George Platis Cadillac on the Eastside started selling more new cars than Fredrick Cadillac of downtown Seattle. Business got so good that George gave his new son-in-law an almost free hand in running the dealership. Soon everybody began to take long vacations, buying mansions, or having them built. The money couldn't be stopped; it flowed into the dealership like the Amazon River.

However, prosperity has a way of changing peoples' priorities. The son-in-law got bored eventually. There were no new mountains to conquer, no new challenges on the horizon, until someone saw him as a new challenge. She was voluptuous beyond belief. Men stopped talking when she came into a room. They did double takes with their heads shaking in disbelief at her natural beauty and gravitated toward her like iron filings to a magnet. Nevertheless, she only had eyes for him. It might have worked itself out eventually, but I doubt it.

People get careless after awhile. They lose their natural caution and overexpose themselves to greater and greater risk. Psychologists theorize that they want to get caught. It lessens their sense of guilt. One fateful night the son-in-law drank a little too much. He took his new conquest to the very posh and quite exclusive Bellevue yacht club. It's too bad, too, because George Platis spotted him there. However, class and breeding won out. George calmly ate his dinner and participated in repartee' with his dinner company. They had an aperitif or two, and then George excused himself and in a direct line walked to his son-in-laws table. Quietly and discreetly he said "I don't want to disturb you, but when you get a chance, stop in and see me on Monday sometime."

Flagarante Delecto the Italians call it. I call it crashing the Mercedes and making the front page of the morning newspaper. (Oh, to have been a fly on the wall.) I'm told George handled it with great decorum and dignity. "I love my daughter and I don't want to see her hurt more than she already has been. Please go away." That is the way the upper class with proper breeding and training handle a gaffe', faux pas, or breech of etiquette, not with smoking guns, and stab wounds to the chest and torso. Unfortunately, not being upper class myself, I most often only get to associate myself with the smoking gun people.

THE TONG

Chinatown became my haunt for a couple of years, at least, until the Tong war broke out. John Leong is the patron head of the Leong Tong. They are the largest and oldest Tong family in Seattle, San Francisco and elsewhere.

The Bing Kung Tong is younger and more militant. They became impatient with the Leong Tong. They wanted excitement. They intercepted a kilo of opium from Vancouver, Canada. A man of respect had it provided for him to finance himself in his new life in America.

Opium is the "gold of gold's" to the Chinese. It can be banked with the Tong. It can be borrowed against. It can be hypothecated. It can be sold. The Bing Kungs' outrageousness had to be redressed. Lots were cast with Mah Jong Tiles to determine who would be the instrument of death.

Willie Mak, Benjamin Ng, and one other individual were selected. They cut thirteen lengths of strong cord to bind their sacrifice. They invaded the Wah Mee club off of a back alley at gunpoint. They tied their thirteen victims and made them kneel down. They fired a 22 bullet behind the ear of each victim. Only one victim lived by feigning death. He recovered at Harbor View hospital under police protection. However, he wouldn't talk to the police. No one in Chinatown would talk to the police. One thing for certain that history has proven is when the bamboo curtain closes nothing goes in or out. I had to get special permission to write these words you are now reading. The men who did the killing fled to Canada, but they are now in police custody.

MARIJUANA

Pete Stayton was a silver-tongued rogue. He could talk the birds down out of the trees. I met him at Rocky Butte jail just outside Portland, Oregon. Rocky Butte was a very interesting place. The inmates had built it. The walls were twenty-two feet thick and quarried out of solid granite. All the cells were sixty-five feet underground. Talk about a prison of your own making. I didn't make it, but I did live in it for seven months while I was waiting to be transported to McNeil Island Federal prison.

Pete was brought into the tank where they were holding one hundred thirty six other prisoners. Maximum capacity of the cell was supposed to be sixty-five people. We had a predominance of black dudes, eighty-one guys, they pretty well bull dogged everyone into doing things their way. Pete grabbed the only bunk that was available; it was next to me.

Over the next seven months I heard his story quite a few times. It started out that he handled every major drug sold from Canada to Baja, California. I allowed a little leeway for sales puffery, or enhancement. By the time he went to court, he was just a courier for very small shipments to California. He worked for a Mediterranean man named Alex. The trouble was Pete wanted to get bigger at his sponsors' expense. I never met a man that had five dollars that didn't want ten.

Pete met two apparently well-connected guys that told him for twenty-two thousand dollars they had customers waiting, and they could turn it into two hundred fifty thousand dollars. They just needed to get their hands on some polypropynol. Pete knew it was a controlled substance used in the manufacture of Methamphetamine. It's called crank, or speed on the street. Washington holds the distinction of being the crank capitol of the United States. The sharp guys kept badgering Pete for the juice, so they could all get rich and retire early. The next thing he knew, they found the polypropynol themselves. They just needed a chemist to cook the juice. Cooking is a highly volatile and very dangerous procedure. One mistake and you can blow everyone to kingdom come. They leaned on Pete, and he caved in. He even invested in the business.

Pete talked his dad into making a twenty-two thousand dollar loan at the bank in his mom's name. She owned the new deluxe doublewide mobile home that they lived in. The dad became convinced big money was right at their fingertips. His daughter's boyfriend Big Larry was to be their protection and muscle if anything went wrong.

They just never imagined how wrong things could go; the local cops had already turned Larry. He was providing steady information on everything he knew on everyone in Grays Harbor, Washington. The DEA (Drug Enforcement Agency) provided a motor home to cook the stuff with. They provided a motor home so they could cook the batch at a rest stop along the 1-5

Interstate corridor. They had the recipe, the Formula and they had Pete. Supposedly they were going to trade the crank for California bud, primo stuff, according to Pete.

Well, Pete cooked all night long and when the morning came they were surrounded by more than two hundred heavily armed law enforcement officers. They were taken into custody. It turned out to not be quite as foolproof as they all thought it was.

Pat almost lost her trailer. The boys had to do some jail time. And Mervyn, the father, became very bitter that he ever got involved. Pete's sister had to put her red dress on, wear her high heels, and go to court to fire their attorney. She retained new counsel and got everything dismissed for entrapment, but it sure was a learning experience for everyone involved. What they learned was "Steady money is better than quick money".

Pete moved to California and worked on a dredging barge for his uncle long enough to have a labor and industries claim. When that ran out, he joined Alcoholics Anonymous and received food stamps, and money for going to meetings every day. He met a girl in the program and they were married. And the last I heard, he had run off with her thirteen-year-old daughter. Pete is forty-three. I heard sometimes those May/ December romances work out, but I wouldn't bet on it.

GIRLS JUST WANT TO HAVE FUN

Not all the players on the criminal cavalcade of stars are men. Sometimes a woman rises to prominence. Abraham Lincoln once made up a little ditty about wayward women when a group of men were actively discussing a girl with round heels, or easy virtue. Approaching the group Lincoln recited, "In spite of what all the hateful fools may say each sniveling, whining yelper, no woman ever went astray without a man to help her." Sometimes the activity may not be criminal, just questionable.

Theresa was born a charmer. Even as a little girl she was cute and quick and liked to be the center of attention. Her mom and Roy her step-dad were long haul over the road truck drivers. They took her along with them for a while. However, eventually it became too difficult to do. They dropped her off with relatives in Minneapolis, and she never forgave them for leaving her behind. In later years she rejoined them. With the addition of sisters and brothers, nobody but mom and dad drove the truck anymore. They were gypsies, or knights of the road as some people term families who travel.

They finally settled in Seattle and rented a house at Angle Lake. It was cool until boredom and alcohol took over. The step-dad was accused of molesting the girls. He went away to Walla Walla Penitentiary. When he got back, he didn't stay with them, but somehow moths are drawn to the flames even if it singes their little angel wings. Daddy and daughter went up to Edmonds and test-drove a BMW at the Saab dealer. They decided they would stay together until the wheels fell off. The wheels fell off sooner than they anticipated. They were apprehended in a Denny's parking lot in San Diego, California. It was an excellent test drive! Dad was apprehended and taken into custody.

Theresa skated the streets of San Diego and panhandled sailors for change. It worked for a year or so, until she met a sailor named Joel.

The Navy, when he wasn't in the brig, taught him welding. They moved in together. Joel got rifted from the Navy and they moved to Conway, Arkansas. They got married when Theresa became pregnant.

When the baby was born she wasn't wanted, so the neighbor took her and adopted her. The neighbor gave Theresa a pick up truck in return. Here is the upshot of this story. The neighbor it turned out had a history of miscarriages and couldn't carry a baby to full term. The new baby's grandma by adoption died shortly thereafter and left her a six hundred and fifty thousand dollars inheritance. Theresa discovered what she didn't want to be and is now in the process of finding out who she does want to be.

There are no perfect people. Look around you and you will see that we are all a work in progress. I learned to reserve judgment for a while and determine what the highest and best use is for every life I come in contact with.

I've often pondered, why can't we have a central registry where babies that aren't wanted could be turned over to the agency in charge and they could be hooked up with parents that want children and for whatever reason are unable to bear them themselves. I presume it's because it is too altruistic and nobody could make enough money from this process.

BULLIES

Once upon a time there was a bully named Buford. He was a red neck from Kentucky. He moved to Ohio. He had a wife and two children. He became the town bartender and he concomitantly became a functioning alcoholic. He worked days in a nearby box factory and ultimately retired from that place after putting in his twenty years. In the meantime, his wife and children were terrified of him. His alcohol fueled despotic rages kept them in line for many years. But his red neck racism and hatred spilled over into everyone's' life until they fled the scene.

His wife had him committed for mental observation for twenty-one days. While he was incarcerated in the hospital, she fled the state with all the money she could get her hands on and moved to Seattle, Washington. Her son and daughter migrated there, also. The son is non-confrontive and amiable. He absorbs abuse until he explodes. He is still trying to win his father's respect. The daughter was very hostile, and angry after years of abuse from men, notably her father and first husband.

One day she had a stroke, or a brain fart, as its known on the street. Her desire to meet everyone else's expectations left her with none of her own. She has greatly recovered from the stroke, but it has left her a kinder and gentler person.

Buford the bully still lives in his tiny town. He is king bullfrog in a very small puddle. But one thing for certain is none of us get out of life alive, and we all live to only inherit a plot of earth six feet by six feet. It isn't so much how we start life, as it is how we finish it. Any of these people aforementioned could have turned to a life of crime. The forces that shape and control us are upon us all. We truly forge ourselves in the fire of our own will.

The opposite of love is not hate it is indifference! There is an old joke that a road repair crew runs over a man with a steamroller.

After prying his identification from his pocket, they take his flattened body to his home. When they arrive there his wife is taking a bath. They knock on the front door and ring the bell. When no one answers, they go through the house-yelling hello until they get a response from the closed door of the bathroom. They tell his wife about the steamroller accident. They want her to identify the body. She responds, "I'm taking a bath right now just slide his body under the door."

The counterpart to that joke is the boy who runs frantically into the front room of the house yelling, "Dad, dad, come quick, mom just fell down the front stairs!"

The dad responds, "Don't make me laugh kid, my lips are chapped." The opposite of love is not hate it is indifference.

As a small boy the first two lessons I consciously remember learning were: you can't love someone you don't trust, and you can't trust someone you don't respect. The second lesson I learned while attending a big pow wow on the reservation. When an Indian got up to talk to the group everyone just kept on talking to their friends, family, and neighbors. When a white man got up to address the group he always had a paper in his hand. Everybody shut up instantly. The paper has power in a credential-oriented society.

When I was twelve years old my foster parents called me into the front room along with my store bought sister. They got her from a different orphanage than they acquired me from. I've found out that only in America do parents think they own their children! They announced that Hazel, our adopted mother, was pregnant, that she had an unexpected accident. We were told that we had to be good or they were taking us back to our respective orphanages.

Alan, who worked for Jimmy Hoffa personally while employed by the union, gave me what I thought was an impossible task. I found out later it was at Hazel's urging. He told me, "You need to bring six hundred dollars per month into the family or you won't be living here anymore."

I complained that I was just a kid and couldn't earn that much money that married guys with a family sometimes didn't make that much.

His response was, "They don't live here with us."

Knowing what I do now, I should have hit the bricks, but instead I learned to hustle. I spent the next several years trying to part the red sea as it were. Well, when I couldn't turn water to wine, or walk across their swimming pool without getting my feet wet, they enforced their desires with whippings. It turned out to be a good thing. I learned I could endure physical punishment and that no matter how expert they got at beating me, they beat more into me than they ever beat out of me. That helped prepare me to box Golden Gloves for the State of California. All I had to do was outlast my opponents. Also, an added benefit was I gained the confidence to know how to survive anywhere.

When I was sentenced to prison my wife said she was leaving me because I would die in there. I laughed and told her, "That's not your real reason. I'm betting my life I won't die in there; I'm a survivor."

Her real reason then tumbled out, "You will never recover from this. You will be ruined financially." She was right, but where she erred was in thinking that her highest priorities were mine. The family meant more to me than any amount of money. I was fired as a husband and father. Oh well, I've been fired before. We all have our share of detractors. If you don't, you aren't trying hard enough. (Smile)

Love Tests: We all have to perform them whether we know it or not. I have an attorney friend who is married to an ex-nun. She writes bad checks and he has to cover them. It's a love test; so far he has always managed to scramble the money together even if he has to borrow it to cover the checks. My wife makes me rearrange my priorities, drop everything I'm doing and take her to lunch. I don't always pass the test. A friend of mine had to divorce his wife and then move back in with her as just a lover and paramour with no formal attachment. So far, he's passing the test. I have another acquaintance that was an inveterate gambler. His father was a drunkard; he has to do whatever his children want him to do to prove his love for them. The flip side is his wife has endured repeated business failures and years of never being able to get ahead financially. She left a hospital after a cancer operation to go back to work so they could pay that months bills. She is still doing it.

I recently checked out of a supermarket line behind two obviously successful yuppie women. They were dressed stylishly in Nordstrom clothes, had their flip cell phones, their appointment organizers in hand, and keys to late model SUV vehicles. One declared to the other that she had nothing special planned for the weekend. She thought she might get married. When queried if it was to the guy she was living with she replied, "yes, I don't really love him, but it is just a starter marriage. I only give it two years tops at most."

It so chilled my heart that I lost my appetite. I put my food back on the shelf. I don't shop at that store anymore; they must have something in their food that removes the heart out of people, or turns it to stone. I rank that with Real Estate Agents that ask, "Hey Indian, do you like the dirt you are standing on?" followed with, "Do you want to buy it?" I realize we all live in a material world and that we are bound by our five senses to inform us of what we see, touch, hear, smell, and feel. Although, just because we can't always take it to the bank doesn't mean it doesn't have value or that it isn't real.

MENDACITY

Every crime begins with a lie. Therein lies the kernel of truth. Our government leaders lie to us and call it disinformation. We lie to our children. We lie to others and our children having learned by example lie back to us. But the relevant issue here lest it get lost in the shuffle is we cannot tell a lie to anyone else without lying to ourselves first. Indeed holy writ indicates that Lucifer, an angel of light, was cast down becoming the Prince of Darkness by adopting the appellation of BELIAL. i.e. (the father of lies} A recent study here in America determined the average American tells three lies a day. I for one am glad that they quantified it because now I can check myself daily to see if I'm running above, or below the average. (Smile)

I am now going to introduce you to two miscreants that are different from each other yet very much the same. Let's see if you can follow the bouncing ball. The first is a man named Tom

F. and the second is a woman named Hannah-Leah, named after two women in the Bible. Both have been married six times. Both have misled their current spouses into believing they are the fourth spouse in their respective marital union. Both were born extra smart. Both have great personal charisma. They have a natural inclination to lead. Both live life on a larger than normal scale of achievement. Both validate themselves by material possessions and high profile accomplishments. Now let me diverge the two.

I met Tom at an interaction transition meeting on Capitol Hill in 1981. Sixty-five ex-convicts were all talking to each other with assorted guests. A very loud basso profundo voice emanating from a three hundred pound man yelled, "Everybody shut up and sit down, please." He began by introducing himself and related that he was a counselor, social worker, minister, facilitator, chorale director, cum business consultant etc. With the hyperbole of a circus barker and the panache of Ed McMann, he led the group down the primrose path.

USERS

I found out later his connection with the group was he was in prison in Idaho for stealing presto logs. He learned quickly. By learning the art of printing in the prison print shop, he discovered he could be anything and anyone he wanted to be. That opened up a world of possibilities to him. He became Jim Rockford from Rockford files. I always enjoyed Rockford's single-minded ingenuity in printing up credentials for getting into any place he wanted to go. Although, Tom was a little scary when he didn't get what he wanted. His gut wrenching yells orchestrated with punching the dashboard, the windows, the doors and anything else in the vicinity tried the courage of most people that dared to challenge, or refuse him. His wrath was awesome to behold.

I drove a 210 Datsun car with him in the dead of winter to South Carolina so he could move there. He had met his sixth woman and married her. She was a highly educated powerful banker. He had hit the mother lode this time. We had a falling out because he would only put five dollars worth of gas in the car at a time. He had induced me to help him by promising to tune the car and pay me one hundred fifty dollars, but I couldn't seem to get the money he owed me. On the road with him, he kept putting me off. He had eight hundred dollars in cash. We kept breaking down and running out of gas. My hegira turned into the Odyssey of Ulysses. He was taught well; whoever controls the money controls everything. I caught a ride back to Washington with him in his wife's CRX Honda. I rode in back with the luggage for ratting him off to his wife that he had opened her new American Express card by intercepting her mail and he had already test driven her card. He tried to abandon me in a little coal town in Wyoming at three a.m. She intervened to stop him.

I watched him put his Grandma in a rest home, and take control of her estate. He transferred the title to himself, and then rented it out to others. He was caught trying to sell a different house he bought in Olympia with a state subsidized loan. They caught it in time because there were liens on the house. So now, if the renters don't pay in a timely manner, he shows up with a six foot ten inches three hundred fifty pound Polish giant named Steve with a forty-five. They always pay. Do I still see the guy? You bet!

We go to violent movies together and go penny ante gambling at Indian casinos. What's not to like? How can you resist a guy that is big, funny, and charming, even when he pees on my shoes and tells me it's raining. But I never, never go out of town with him anymore, and I always have an escape plan. If you like the faint smell of cordite gunpowder in the air and enjoy the antics of a charismatic rogue at play, Tom Fairchild is your man. He is a living three-ring circus.

PROFESSIONALISM

Hannah-Leah was born in Bellingham, Washington. She was attractive and an over achiever and smarter than everyone else she came in contact with. In high school she excelled. She walked away with all the top awards and honors.

Somehow she figured out the shortest path between two points is not a straight line necessarily. You can marry someone who is already where you want to be. Five husbands later the men's money was gone and so was she. She is a licensed realtor, licensed helicopter pilot, business broker, and International traveler. She quickly discovered if you own a business outside this country and if it goes belly up there are no taxes. No one can complain and you can create a new entity. She entertains lavishly. She does business on a grand scale.

Example: You rent a Boeing 747 airplane. Rent a pilot. Fill the airplane with pharmaceuticals with expired dates and fly it to Tashkent, Uzbekistan, or Kebekastan. You sell the drugs for cash. Then you fly Russian Jews to Israel for a high fee, having convinced them there are jobs and housing available. You drop your load, wing home to Seattle. Pay the pilot off and start a new project.

Meanwhile Safeco Insurance Company was paying for her mother unbeknownst to them to be her home care nurse. They believed she was sick; meanwhile, she's jetting around the world. The insurance company pays everybody, and everything. Her husband earns one point two million dollars in a year, and she spends one point three million, a year. Didn't I tell you she was smarter than everyone else? Who says you can't squeeze blood out of a stone? It still begs the question. Is she bad, or just smarter than everyone else? I don't know the answer to that conundrum. Without a doubt, she is preeminently successful.

MASTER CON MAN

I met a man named Howard Pellet. Howard is now a retired I.R.S. agent whose specialty was corporate fraud. He told me one day "I'm not interested in the salesman who pads his travel expenses, nor am I interested in the trucker who shaves his truck log, or charges off a lunch. I am a wolf catcher. I want the big bad wolf." He continued with, "My problem isn't really with the wolf, it lies with the sheep. Most people are sheep. When I catch the wolf and put him away the sheep get nervous and they mill around until they find another wolf, or they create another wolf." I thought him rather cynical at the time, but I have revised my opinion of his statement and concur it may be so.

I now want to introduce you to the greatest rogue I have ever met. He is still at large. He says that he will never be caught because he is too smart to ever fall. Howard Pellet tried to bring him down for twenty-two years, but finally gave up because the clock ran out of time.

Before I tell you his name and how he runs his game, I want to warn you that Satan doesn't wear seersucker. He comes at you refined, cool, poised, and in control. A true sociopath doesn't have a conscience.

That said; let me introduce you to the Devil's Advocate...Dean Kalevas. Dean is a tax attorney. He is licensed to practice tax law. If you believe his letterhead, he has offices in Washington D.C., Zurich, Switzerland, the Cayman Islands, and Washington State. Try to find his offices if you can. They are only letter drops. If you call the International phone number, he will screen the call and call you back. No matter where you, are he will meet you somewhere of mutual convenience. When you do hook up with him you will find him handsome, suave, urbane, polished, confident, and utterly convincing. He perceives he is a Renaissance man. He is learned in art, music, law, and medicine. He works out in an exclusive athletic club in Seattle, upper body three days a week and lower body three days a week, one day for recovery. He is highly disciplined, and punctilious to a fault, especially if you are an attractive female.

Dean Kalevas is one charismatic rogue. He has successfully stolen over one hundred million dollars. Dean worships the golden age of Greece and is certain he could have been Emperor if he had lived then. He may be right. He carries himself with grace and ease. He knows food, and wine intimately. He knows the finest places to shop anywhere in the world. He eats at the finest restaurants in major Metropolitan cities. And most of all, he never pays taxes to anybody. You see Dean doesn't own anything. He has no real property, not in his name anyway. Women and investors pay for Dean to live the way he does. He is the first to point out that women are a distinct class of supporters, separate from investors in general.

Here is how the drill works...You meet somewhere with Dean by appointment, preferably over food, but I've known him to do a deal over a golf game. Incidentally, if you are a scratch golfer he will let you win by a stroke or two. However, if there is money bet i.e. a thousand dollars a hole or more go home and get your deed because while you were out plowing the south forty acres, Dean bought your farm. He is that good at virtually everything he does! His art taste is exquisite and it always appreciates in value.

Casually, Dean will ask you over bread and wine, "Are you ever tired of paying taxes?"

The mark, or pigeon usually replies, "Isn't everyone?"

Dean's sense of timing is exquisitely honed. "You don't have to pay taxes anymore if you don't want to. From today on you will be among the elite upper class rich people I represent that never pay a penny in income taxes."

The mark usually asks, "State, or Federal?"

Dean replies, "Both."

The hook is in big time. Inevitably the sucker asks, "How is that possible?"

Answer, "I form a corporation, it is a separate entity from either you or me. Let's say just for the sake of discussion, I put one million dollars into the corporation and you match it with one million dollars. We now have jointly funded our corporate entity. Of course I've drawn up all the necessary paperwork to make sure everything is done perfectly legal. I will assume total tax liability personally for everything; I'll do all the necessary filings required by law. I will take the corporation outside the Continental United States to the Bahamas or form it outside the United States if you prefer. I'll open a numbered account in Zurich, Switzerland. Only you and I will know about it and have access to it. I already have offices in Switzerland. We then have two million dollars at our disposal to take advantage of any extraordinary business opportunities that may arise. Other countries are paying exceptionally high interest rates for the use of American dollars, sometimes as much as a thousand percent. United States laws do not govern them.

The mark usually has dollar signs in his eyes and asks, "Is that legal?"

"It is the way I do it" is the reply. "I haven't paid a penny in taxes for over thirty years now, neither do any of my clients."

If the Mark bolts, or gets nervous about the amount, Dean gets nonchalant. "If a million is too rich for your blood how much do you want to put into it initially? Remember it's matching dollars. Whatever you put in, I'll match it. Once the initial equity is funded, it is self-perpetuating. So, how soon do you want to get started?" As he talks Dean draws diagrams on napkins. He always picks up the napkin and the check.

One greedy man vested his entity with twelve million dollars. Another greed stricken fool let Dean pick the corporate entity name. He didn't realize ALUCARD backwards is DRACULA until the money was all gone into Dean's personal legal account. That usually happened within twenty-four hours from the deposit of the mark's money. It made a sitting judge in Tacoma furious, but there wasn't a thing the loser could do to recover against Dean. He doesn't own anything in his own name. A judge in Canada was outraged that a Canadian entity formed by Dean named BLACKSTONE was nothing but a conduit.

Dean's response when he appeared in court was, "I named it that after the famous Supreme Court Judge Justice Blackstone." I noted there was also a famous magician named Blackstone. Evidently the judge didn't snap to that until it was way too late. The money was long gone.

Dean got me for twenty two thousand dollars, which he told me he would never pay. I got him a real estate loan for seven hundred fifty thousand dollars. His excuse to me was you got the loan commitment from my bank; I won't ever pay for a bank I'm already doing business with. I pointed out that they turned him down when he applied on his own. I had to bring in a heavy hitter with a financial profile like a rock to make the thing take off. He won! I'm still licking my wounds. However, I really liked the day he was arrested while he was paying a fellow attorney for the use of his conference room. He gave him some cash to say he consulted to their firm and had offices there. While Dean was setting the stage in the conference room, two cops busted through to arrest him for one hundred sixty-seven unpaid parking tickets that he had accumulated with other peoples' cars.

Dean was screaming, "Don't cuff me in front of my client, if you do, I'll have your badge, I have friends in high places. This is chump change; I could buy and sell both of you guys a hundred times over."

One cop told him as they led him out of the building, "Save your money pal, you are going to need it to make bail." I know this because one of his ladies at the moment wrote the check to get him out of jail, and I was the mule that carried it to the courthouse for her! It was too funny. But so far Dean Kalevas has made a believer out of me, that if you are ruthless enough and can capitalize on other peoples' weakness you can accumulate a hell of a lot of money. He proved it; he is still at large and in charge.

One of my favorite stories is…A guy goes to his neighbor to borrow his axe. His neighbor says, "I can't loan you my axe right now because I'm making soup."

"What does making soup have to do with borrowing your axe?"

His neighbor said, "Nothing at all, but if I don't want to loan you my axe, one excuse is as good as another."

I have found that all criminals have a reason for their criminal behavior. It's never their fault. They were misunderstood as a child, or society disappointed them, or someone let them down. Bullshit! You don't have to flip a cow pie over to know its bullshit on the other side, too. We need to spend less time looking for mitigating circumstances and get people to accept responsibility for their own behavior.

POLITICS & MONEY

An attorney I know called me and said he had a client that needed special help. He wanted me to meet with them in a special place that he didn't want to disclose over the phone. I agreed to meet them and went there straight away. When I got there he was trying to calm a hysterical female dressed to the nines with a big straw hat and dark glasses. Obviously the lady was terrified. She then told me her story. It surprised me. I didn't think I could be surprised by anybody anymore.

Her husband was a major politician in Olympia. They had the house by the sea with Jamaican servants, a helicopter pad etc. He had tried to kill her and darn near succeeded. She was in hiding. It seems the husband gave a check to an L.A. coin dealer for eight hundred forty thousand dollars for Mexican gold coins, uncirculated 50 Peso pieces. They were worth twelve hundred twenty dollars each.

Simultaneously he slipped another Los Angeles coin dealer a check for four hundred ten thousand dollars for Mexican 50 Peso uncirculated gold pieces. All of this happened on a Friday night after the banks closed on the eve of a three-day holiday. The husband hired two gypsy jokers from their motorcycle gang to take the coins to a drop in a San Diego bank. They did the delivery and returned to Olympia to be paid. They received their money and one of them took off.

The other stayed to do some excellent ninety two percent pure cocaine. The politician had cut it with Manitol, a baby laxative, as opposed to milk sugar and he wanted to unload it fast. The gypsy joker was hired to drive it to the Tacoma bus station and store it in a wall locker and bring the key to him. The joker completed the task and disappeared.

Meanwhile the politician had addicted his wife to the Peruvian Jungle Juice and he had left a note where she would be sure to find it. You might have noticed drug addicts do not always think very rationally. She thought she had found an endless supply of Mother's Little Helper. She turned the place upside down and tossed the place so it would look like a burglary. She found the locker key from the bus depot. The only thing that saved her life is she called the gypsy joker who put it there, to take her to do the pick up. She had the key in the locker and was just getting ready to turn it, when the Joker saw the wire clippings on the ground. He had been to Viet Nam. He knew what that meant. He grabbed her in a vise like grip just in the nick of time.

Later after an anonymous phone call, the Washington Bomb squad opened the locker very carefully. There were enough explosives in that locker with both a trip fuse, and C-4 plastique that could be set off by microwave to blow Tacoma to Canada. She did the right thing. As they used to say in cowboy days, "She got out of Dodge City." We didn't let her go home to pack. Meanwhile, the politician kidnapped his two daughters by luring them on a promised trip to Mexico with him.

He just didn't tell them that he was the only one coming back. My assignment was to find the motorcycle man and induce him to testify.

Now the story becomes real interesting. Lo and behold, Dean Kalevas shows up at the San Diego bank and takes delivery of all the coins. He transports them to Switzerland. He returns with a numbered bank account card. Only the politician and Dean had access to the account. The story gets a little muddy now because Dean alleges the guy lost the account number. The guy alleges Dean gave him a phony account number. I tell the wife to employ J.J. Arms of San Francisco to go to Mexico and kidnap her daughters back. He always is for hire for the right amount of money and he always retrieves the hostages no matter how difficult it is. He never fails his clients.

Meanwhile, Mr. politician had two very intense and dedicated men kidnap Dean Kalevas and take him to an out of the way motel room where they proceeded to torture him. After three days of torture, Dean is getting tired. Tough as he is, anyone can be broken if the right techniques are employed. He agrees to go to Switzerland and retrieve the money. I had to admire his courage under very difficult circumstances. It is hard to hold your mud as they say in the construction industry when the whole wall is threatening to collapse on you. Dean finally convinced them that if they killed him they got zero, and one hundred percent of nothing is nothing. Dean paid off the politician. He is alive and well and so is the wife.

I found the gypsy Joker living in a furniture store in Tacoma. His momma gave him up to me when I convinced her I was a friend of his that owed him money and he could probably use a few bucks. She agreed he needed some money. The tricky part was negotiating the affidavit in a gypsy joker clubhouse with my attorney friend and myself and a very suspicious biker gang. However, that's another story for another time perhaps.

Incidentally, the divorce was handled quietly. The girls returned to Tacoma and both of them graduated from high school with the rest of their friends. Sometimes it's hard to tell friend from foe, so it helps to reserve judgment until everybody sorts themselves out. I have a friend who says, "It was easier in Viet-Nam; anyone that came at me with a gun, I killed them and let God sort them out later.

My Viet Nam friend can fix anything. He now works as a mechanic on Mercer Island repairing the cars of the very rich people. It's good work if you can get it. In Viet Nam as a 17-year-old kid they made him a helicopter repairman. They had a unique incentive program. He had to fly in any airplane he worked on. Helicopters are notably unforgiving of human error. It motivated him, as he puts it, "Not to have too many bring backs!" He prides himself on not having bring backs with the cars he works on, but when he first got back to Seattle, he had a little trouble understanding how to turn off the killing machine. It's hard when your country sends you to be cannon fodder because you are an "expendable item" and if you die it's an "acceptable, number." So one day you're killing anyone you are pointed to and the next day someone says, "No more killing, quit it!"

Two black guys thought they would pistol whip and rob him downtown in Pioneer square late one night. He found out too late that he hadn't quite mastered the part about not killing anymore. The judge was lenient because there were witnesses. However, he adjured him and admonished him to not carry a gun anymore. So he doesn't carry guns anymore.

He has a pit bull instead. The pit bull is named Shapiro. It eats grapes, celery, olives, cucumbers or anything else that Dave eats. He'll do anything for him. The last words some miscreants ever hear is, "Eat em Shupe." I made friends with the dog first and its master later. I've been trying to train my wife's Shit-Tzu to be that attentive, but all he wants to do is invite the bad guys in so they will give him a treat and have a party.

NAVY KILLERS

A friend of mine called with a business proposal. A Jew, an Atheist, and a Mormon wanted me to sell some Parchment scroll manuscripts for them. I looked their stuff over and I was suitably impressed. It was first-rate merchandise. We had the meeting. I explained all I do is get orders. You guys fill them. I get paid up front, or you can forget it. I take a draw every Monday against the orders I've placed. I don't ever want to hear a sob story, or an excuse. I will never be involved in production even if the sky is falling and the world is going to end. I'm not worried about my end. My end is a done deal; it's your end that worries me. Can you deliver? They said YES. I took the job.

Within one month I had eight hundred confirmed orders. I had them qualified to go into the Lillian Carter and Walter Drake catalog for cash. The catalogs would buy, warehouse and distribute the merchandise. My guys started sniveling and whining, and making excuses.

Steve Lidstrom, the Atheist accountant, and Ted the Psychotic Jew it seems had run dark operations for the Navy in Viet Nam. They wanted me to repay my draw to them, or they would kill me. Now that was the kind of language that gets my full attention and makes my pilot light turn on. Thereafter, it went to full flame. They bragged that they had killed over four hundred people in Cambodia, and Viet Nam and one more didn't matter to them. I told them I wasn't very impressed. The four hundred unarmed men, women and children killed with automatic machine guns wasn't much of a fight. They then started making threatening phone calls to kill my wife and child.

Well, they killed someone, but it wasn't who they expected. They jointly owned a convalescent home with six patients. Ted was married to a Filipino woman that was a nurse. Two of their patients died in the next sixty days. It seems their night nurse was a drunk and one of the patients choked to death on a pill too large to swallow.

Another patient died because the same nurse nodded off and one of the patients who was critical couldn't rouse her from her Rip Van Winkle sleep. The last I heard, Howard Pellet, the wolf catcher, and the State of Washington Health Department were hot on their trail. An ancient Chinese curse was: "May you live in interesting times."

There can be more than one way to skin a cat. Steve's wife found another guy, some ballet dude she spends the night with. To me that is just tutu perfect. Ted, the psychotic, takes enough narcotics to stop a train. He threatened to kill his neighbor for doing him a favor and pulled his gun on another neighbor for cutting his grass for him.

I guess their street won't be eligible to win "The Street of Dreams" or "Parade of Homes" this year. Frank Sinatra updated this when he said, "Sometimes life is a kick in the head".

Shakespeare covered the subject of good and evil by having Marc Anthony deliver a powerful eulogy at the funeral of Julius Caesar. "The evil that men do oft lives after them, the good is interred with their bones." No one has ever said it better than that.

SPIDER MAN

Jim Feeney was the original Spiderman. I discovered in my travels that anything that was poisonous or deadly lived in Australia. No wonder those Aussies are such a tough lot.

We forget that this world is seventy three percent water and there are seven floating landmasses we call continents. I had to visit the seven continents because when you sell money for a living, the element of greed is a universal appetite and it brings every con man and hustler right to your door. I liken it to picking birdseed out of horse manure. You have to choose very carefully. Usually if someone has a worthy project to finance, a bank, a savings and loan, or an insurance company gobbles them up.

I made it a practice to give a rote speech to every wanna be client. It went something like this: "I don't know why you chose us to represent you, but you need to know several things before we sign any paperwork committing either of us to anything. We don't have any money and we don't write the check. We are mortgage brokers not mortgage bankers. My job is to screen you out. I am more interested in the lender than you. He has the money, you don't, or you wouldn't be talking to us. We are the bottom of the barrel. No one in their right mind would come to us, and pay us a fee for getting them a loan if they could get the loan themselves without our fee. We have no guarantee except we will all die someday. Nobody gets out of life alive. All we can do is make a best efforts appeal to as many lenders that will let us submit your project to them. The rest is up to them. Most are turned down; very few get funded. Characteristically, less than five percent are ever funded, or you wouldn't be here."

Here' s what the clients testified to in court. (after much coaching by the F.B.I. and the prosecutor) "Those guys swore on their mother's graves, and their children's eyes that they had the money in the bank in a passbook savings account and they were going to give it to me because they liked my face and my attitude. So I gave them a retainer fee and they ripped me off. I didn't get funded at the rate, or terms I wanted or I didn't get as much money as I expected. I forgot about their one percent fee etc."

I don't watch much T.V. but when I do, I like Discovery channel or National Geographic. They are real! I have enough fantasy in my life already with the politics, preachers and the infomercials. One day I tuned in to the discovery channel and they were whispering as some guy in shorts with a pencil poked it into a funnel shaped spiders web. The narrator exclaimed in a hushed monotone, "If this fellow bites you, it's all over for you. You won't live long enough to receive medical attention. There is no known antidote. It's venom is so potent one drop could kill a herd of elephants, charging rhinos, a flock of zebras, and everybody you know and everything you love.

Wow! That got my attention. It turns out he exaggerated his claim just a little, but I guessed that it was just sales puffery or a mild enhancement. I thought about the idiot sticking the pencil in the web and felt sorry for him. It didn't seem very safe, or like a very good thing to do. Just then this nasty looking spider the size of a mans hand came rushing out of his funnel web and bites the crap out of the pencil. He was squirting venom and shaking the pencil. If spiders roar, this guy was roaring.

The narrator says, "There it is, the funnel web spider, the most deadly creature on earth drop for drop. Pound for pound he makes a king cobra look like a child's plaything. I agreed with him. It convinced me I am never going to Australia slipping on a pair of shorts and going for a walk about in the outback with only a pencil to defend myself. I'm not going to be poking my pencil into funnel web spider's nests just to see if they are home. I got to thinking about that spider and how he spun that funnel web one strand at a time until he had a place of concealment from which to ambush unsuspecting prey, which in the spider's case was mice, lizards, birds, snakes, or anything it could overpower.

It reminded me of Jim Feeney, the smoothest, slickest, most convincing con man I have ever known and met in my short life. To know him is to love him. Let me introduce him to you...But be sure and count your fingers after you shake hands with him.

REINSTATEMENT

I had served three years in federal prison for mail and wire fraud conspiracy. I then served six months in a half way house, two years parole, then two years probation. I never had any other incidents. Therefore my time was up. Seven and a half years gone when the world flipped right side up again.

I received an official letter from Judge Robert Burns, my sitting senior Judge for the ninth circuit court that presided over my case. It said in short..."Your time is served, you've paid your debt to society, you can go back to being a finance and mortgage broker again." I always puzzled over why they had never taken my securities license, or my cryptography clearance. I just presumed it was because they would cancel me out if I reapplied to work in those fields again. It didn't have much meaning for me because I had a job. I worked every day. I got paid. That's all I wanted from then on. Once you crash and burn in the Rockies, you don't go flying again.

A very smart attorney I knew thought otherwise. I explained to him I didn't have a death wish. I had made eighty-four parachute jumps; that was enough. I didn't need the metallic taste of adrenaline on my tongue anymore. I got over that. I didn't want to be kamikaze pilot with only one mission and enough fuel to fly only one way. I wanted to be a kamikaze with twenty-nine missions, involved, but not committed. He convinced me after several months that we could keep our day jobs and only take loan proposals that we could do. He would screen everything himself and protect us both. He would be the only one to touch the money, if there was any, and he would assume all fiduciary responsibility. The guy was honest and I trusted him so I took a chance on him.

Well it's funny, you drop a penny into a pond and the penny disappears, but the ripples continue into the eternities. People started coming to us out of the woodwork. Seattle may be a metropolitan city, but everybody drinks out of the same well. Banks started calling us to get them deals they could do and clients did, too. We only took the real estate ones the banks could do.

I'd asked the F.B.I. boys why they came after me in the Nationwide Funding case when they had illegally tapped my phone for two years, subpoenaed my bank records, and knew I didn't have the two hundred twenty eight million dollars. They said, "It wasn't about the money, it was insured anyway." Then what was it about I wanted to know? Their reply fractured me; "It wasn't anything personal, you just happened to be in the wrong place at the wrong time." It sure seemed real personal to me. (Smile)

Well, we stumbled along trying to earn a bowl of rice as my Chinese friends say, when I got the call. Bobby Lott called me and said, "I've got a Swiss Bank that guarantees one hundred percent of any loan you would like to make. I expressed my disbelief. Bobby said, "Meet me at

Girvan's' on the waterfront tomorrow night; bring your attorney friend and bring a date. Jim Feeney is coming into town.

Wow! Bobby was no slacker when it came to entertaining. Girvan's' was the nicest restaurant in Seattle. It overlooked Elliott Bay and you could watch the ships while you ate dinner. Canlis had great food too but Roger Girvan had live Maine Lobster flown in daily, my all time favorite food, but not one that crawled onto my table or perched on my plate very often. Of course, it goes without saying, I went to dinner. Well, the rest is history. Jim Feeney rolled into that restaurant and took it like Grant took Richmond. He was like a visiting prince. He had the Swiss air about him and the haughty demeanor of someone who knows by birth he is born better than everyone else he will ever meet in this lifetime. He was dressed in a fifteen hundred Barzoni suit, hand cut with single needle tailoring. The shoes were wafer thin, obviously special order hand cut Gucci leather, the watch was a wafer thin Patek Philippe, the ring a first water Ceylon Star Sapphire. He had it all going on for him. We had some appetizers, calamari and stuffed mushrooms while they got our table ready for us. Bobby's date confused squid tentacles with testicles, but since her bust line was bigger than her I.Q. it didn't matter. I understand they went hot tubbing later and he clarified it for her.

After our table was made ready, we sat and ordered dinner. Jim Feeney took center stage. The dog and pony show was marvelous. He was a gifted ringmaster and boy was it ever a three ring circus. There was a lot going on in the old big top that night. I've always enjoyed a good carnival, especially the freak show. Only, we were the freaks on display for the world to see. Jim ran his broken field run and it was a real razzle-dazzle play. He was married to a Swiss citizen. He had dual citizenship; Swiss law did not affect any business transacted off Swiss soil. He regaled us with stories of people he knew like

Bernie Cornfeld who broke Swiss law and was imprisoned in a Swiss castle for awhile. (Bernie's party girl Victoria Principal, Robert Vesco that took one hundred million dollars and fled to Costa Rica.)

The long and the short of it all was he had a portfolio of loan guarantees of major stock firms, insurance companies, Prime Federal banks, and most of all, he was on the board of a major Swiss private Bank, Aubert & Cie, that had been in business for two hundred years. It was an answer to every lenders prayers. Now my associate and I had lost some deals that we could have made if we had those kinds of assurances. So as Ross Perot would have said "I'm all ears."

When I challenged the validity of his representations and the veracity of the truthfulness of his documents, I watched his eyes and they didn't even flicker. The guy was good, real good! He never missed a beat when my attorney friend asked for references and proof of past performance in the United States and not abroad; he just smiled and reached into his attaché and produced the appropriate "Bona Fides" without any hesitation. It didn't cause him to break stride at all.

We had lost two deals to the United States Government. One was a way to check peoples' inner eye to identify them. It was "Eye Identify" and the other was a remote surveillance drone airplane with live feed television. We were still smarting over it because as soon as we had written commitments from Barclays Bank, the Government took everything away from us. With the kind of assurances Jim Feeney was purporting to have, we could do bigger and better projects. We could reject the riff raff from the outset and only deal with la crème' de la crème'. We finished the dinner and went home. The next day we checked all the references and everything checked.

Well, we got lucky. We didn't do any business with Jim Feeney, but we heard reports that some lucky suckers did. From what we heard, they put up huge cash deposits and lost them.   Supposedly they were escrowed with every caveat and contingency built in the marks could think of. Big Jim got their money. In effect they invested in a gold mine with proven reserves. Jim got the gold and they got the shaft.   It wouldn't have been found out for a long time to come, but Pierre Aubert died suddenly.   They closed the Aubert & Cie bank for audit and inventory.   By the way, Jim Feeney wasn't on their board, not even remotely associated was the way the Swiss explained it to me. No wonder the Swiss have the strongest currency in the world; ninety-seven percent of their currency is backed by hard precious metals.

Any country that can convince the rest of the world that while Hitler is taking control of the world we remained neutral has my respect. After the war they amended that first report with we did let Adolph and a few of his friends store some things here. Followed with we did negotiate a few personal loans for them and some cash advances. However, we didn't know they were using it for rockets, bombs, airplanes, or all that. They say the difference between rape and rapture is salesmanship. If anyone buys into the Swiss we were neutral while super powers fought for world domination. I have a great little condominium in Iraq with some swell beachfront property they can stay at.

Well, Jim Feeney suddenly disappeared. As Abraham Lincoln once commented, "the story loses nothing in the telling." I heard he got a slap on the wrist and spent a few months in jail on United States soil it seems the Swiss were embarrassed by his representations and activities. The last I heard was when I got a call from Florida. It seems the Federales convinced him to work off his debt by doing stings for them in Florida and Arizona. I know this, no matter how sincere he seems I wouldn't let him baby-sit my kids, or escort my wife to the opera.

SATAN'S HIGH PRIEST

Once upon a time in a land far away there was a place called California where I had decided to get rich. Evidently, I wasn't the only one that decided that California was the land of golden opportunity. Everybody I met there wanted to be richer than everyone else. The aerospace industry was booming. The Kennedy's were in power and the United States economy was a run away train. Everything looked golden.

It was summertime in California and I was working two jobs so I could save lots of money and then go away to Utah where I had a scholarship for the fall semester of school. I was supposed to get a degree that would be my guaranteed passport to happiness. Then I could go live in Happy Valley with all the other successful people, get married, have two cars, 1.5 children, and live happily ever after.

On the weekends I had to do my laundry and other domestic chores that piled up while I was working. My laundry turned out to be my favorite chore. It was next to a topless dance place called the *"Outrigger."* I could watch two partially clad nubile young women simulate sexual ecstasy while my clothes churned away next door. Then I could watch two more nubile young sirens shimmy while my clothes did the Saint Vitus dance in the big commercial dryer adjacent to me. It almost made housework seem enjoyable.

One night while I was discharging my domestic duties, I saw a big bald headed guy in a leather coat talking to the dancers on stage. He whispered, so I couldn't hear what he said to them. Some of them seemed eager to talk to him. He handed one hundred dollar bills to the ones that nodded yes to him. I approached one of the dancers and asked about him. She seemed scared. Her reaction kind of surprised me. I thought she would say he was arranging a private party or something like that. Instead, she said, "Don't you know who that is?"

I said "No"

She said, "He is Antoine Lavey; he's Satan's high priest."

I laughed! "Surely you don't believe that do you?"

"Oh yes I do," she replied "he can do stuff no other human I know can do. He can summon Satan, or curse you if he chooses to; I've seen him do it."

At the time, Charley Manson and his helter skelter bunch were running around scaring and killing people and I knew people were weirded out over that and not acting rational anymore. So I blew it off and went home. The newspapers had something about the rat pack with Frank Sinatra and his pals, Jane Mansfield, and other Hollywood people crowding the news every day. I figured I'm only going to be in California two more months, and then I'm off to college and the desert and mountains of Utah. I won't have to deal with these people ever again. I figured I'd never see any of them again and it would all be just a dim memory. Boy, was I wrong.

In my travels I ran into a guy I used to go to high school with. We were even in the boy scouts together. Paul was now a successful stock analyst for Dempsey Tegler a big firm in downtown Los Angeles. He seemed glad to see me and suggested we hook up and go dancing at "The Daisey" and "The Factory." His clients could get us in the door. They were the happening places at the time so I agreed to do the town with him and his wife. I got a date and we drove down to lala land in downtown L.A. Neither of us drank alcohol so I didn't have to worry about either of us driving home.

We were at the second club when I saw Antoine Lavey doing what looked like a mating dance with a girl dressed in black leather that was so tight it left nothing to the imagination. It looked like she bought it when she was five years old and she just kept growing into it. She was the most voluptuous woman I had ever seen. I was captivated. They were fondling and hugging each other in places I didn't know existed. If I was going to go blind for looking I had to risk one eye. Paul, his wife, my date and I sat down and ordered lemonade; it was very hot in there.

Imagine my surprise when I looked up and miss naughty pants was standing in front of me. She asked me to dance. I hesitated, but my date said I could go if I remembered the way home if I got lost. I was already lost. I just didn't know it yet! We danced and tried to talk to each other over the cacophony of sound. She said her name was Leda the Black Swan. I noticed the pupils of her eyes were huge and dilated like a cats at midnight. I made a mental note that only three drugs LSD, atropine, and belladonna made your pupils expand that large. Every other drug makes your pupils smaller, even pinpoint in size. She was California tripping, solo I thought.

"Where is the guy I saw trying to father your children that you were dancing with earlier?" I asked.

She thought that was very funny. "Antoine really is my father" she exclaimed.

"Metaphorically or literally?" I wanted to know.

"Both," she replied.

I was stunned. I kept trying to flee her, but she held me fast with her eyes, her arms and every other part of her. I was caught like a fly in a web, or a moth around a flame. I forgot I had friends, my date, or anything but her. It wasn't until the music stopped that I came to my senses again. I had to say goodbye to Leda and Fantasyland and go back to the real world. We left and it was over.

A few weeks later, Charley Manson and his crew of space cadets got caught. Jane Mansfield got her head cut off in a freak automobile accident and the word went out that it was because Antoine Lavey had cursed her. It seems that he had promoted her career. Afterwards she had used her considerable talents to promote herself further. Then she cruelly dumped him. Some guys are sore losers. He struck me as that type. Maybe he did curse her, but I didn't think so.

I moved to Utah and went to school. I later worked out a sweat equity to buy an interest in a Baskin Robbins ice cream franchise. In time I found an Idaho farm girl who fell off the sugar beet truck and rolled into Utah. I picked her up, dusted her off and married her. Years passed, we worked and worked. We made babies. We bought stuff and we went to more schools. We went to church. We raised our little carpet commandos, our tiny little curtain climbers. We made lots of trips to the dairy farm in Idaho. I wandered around in dungarees asking her dad which end of the cow should I milk now, while she went shopping with her mom.

But then it happened, the impossible came out of nowhere and blindsided me. It was one of those late night calls that chills your blood and makes you want to tell the other party this is a wrong number and hang up. A man I knew with twelve kids who was a faithful Mormon bishop from Nevada told me Satan is in Utah.

I said, "He's everywhere, so what."

He didn't think that was too funny. "I'm not kidding," he said. "He has sixty three Mormon kids trapped in a boarded up church and he's trying to get some more to take with him."

"To where?" I asked, thinking he was going to respond with hell, Hades, Sheol, ghenna, the nether world, or something like that.

Instead he said, "Oakland, California."

I was getting ready to tell him it was probably a fig newton of his imagination, but something in his voice told me he wasn't kidding. He was scared, real scared.

He then said, "I already made an appointment with Satan for midnight; I gave him your name and told him that you and I would fight him for those kids."

I said "Will, you're crazy, I don't do that kind of stuff anymore. You need an apostle, an opossum or Moses and Aaron. I'm none of the above."

He begged me to go, so I went. There was nothing good on T.V. that late at night, anyway. Well, we went to meet the Devil, but lo and behold, it was just Antoine Lavey and his daughter Leda the Black Swan. It seems like she had more than one role to play in his eternal scheme of things. I noticed the kids were all drugged into insensibility. He had tricked them by altering reality with candles and drugs, and a bunch of mumbo jumbo any stage magician could do. Will and I turned the lights on and the illusion was broken. All that in the dark stuff doesn't work real good in the light. Things in life are not always the way they appear to be. Life is uncertain so you should always eat your dessert first. Will and I took the kids to their parents.

However, before we left I explained to Antoine and his daughter that they needed to look for another line of work. The one they were pursuing seemed to have some real pit falls in it.

They didn't thank me for sharing so I elucidated further. "Only God has true power, all others have to get it from him. You're worshipping an illusion.

Anciently it was called the mirror hand or the sinister hand. It didn't work well for the Egyptian magicians that opposed Moses and it obviously isn't working very well for you guys. It's time for you to go home, and while you are at it, you should repent of the evil you are trying to do because you are not very good at it. Satan should fire you for incompetence. You guys can't even conjure up a good curse, spell, or incantation. A curse is only the interruption of a blessing. Big deal, most people curse themselves and make it a self-full filling prophecy.

They went back to Oakland, California and their black castle. Antoine Lavey passed away on Halloween night. What a wonderful irony, I almost died laughing. Satan had fully vested his 401(K) retirement program with death. What a fabulous pay off. It's funny but you lose some of your fear of the unknown with education and experience.

PAST HAPPINESS

I had moved to Happy Valley Utah, where like the mythical land of Camelot everything was bliss. Even though it was a desert kingdom, it had some redeeming features. For one thing it was the polar extreme of California. Utah people had lots of education, but very little cash. California had become the Sodom and Gomorrah of its day. Los Angeles and San Francisco were twin sister cities dedicated to greed and lust. Everybody I met there was from somewhere else. They had just migrated there to catch the tail end of the gold rush, as soon as they struck the big one, the mother lode, the main vein; they were headed out with their riches in tow. Funny thing though, California gold can be real elusive. I didn't strike it rich in California, but I found if I worked for very little money and didn't demand too much in return, everybody wanted to hire me. Entry-level positions were begging to be filled. The guys who live by the golden rule, he who has the gold makes the rules, discovered if you could get people to value themselves at zero, the sky is the limit to what you can accomplish.

I thought Utah would be different, so I emigrated. I now playfully believe Plymouth Rock should have landed on the Pilgrims or maybe the North American Indians should have banned immigration. I have a reservation, but it's about the white mans' system of counting coup. I let a guy that befriended me convince me that Utah played by different rules.

This guy could sell sand to Arabs, snow to Eskimos, and blue sky to the birds. His name was Lamar, I later found out his system consisted of buying a little of everything that someone else was selling. If any of them made money, you might make some, too. In the valley of the blind the one eyed man is King. My friend had seventy five thousand dollars cash, a big house to sell, and a chiropractic practice in Hollywood. He looked like a king to me. He convinced me I didn't need any money to move to Utah. I could pay with a smile, and live on faith. He was right. It worked real well for him. I took a job working a sweat equity for Baskin Robbins Ice Cream. He gave me a quasi title: The Head Scooper, the guy in charge, a white knight (cuz you had to wear all white uniforms including a little white paper hat. I answered to head puba or my man, my boy, boss guy, or manager, whatever he was in the mood to call me.

Whenever I complained and reminded him that raising a wife, two kids, and myself on six hundred fifty dollars a month wasn't what I moved to Utah for, he would do his sackcloth and ashes routine, tear his hair and cry out aloud, "I gave you a raise. We only have five stores. I have big expenses; I bought two boats and seven cars last year because I have a big family. I don't even take a salary. You have a guaranteed income. What I wouldn't give to have that blessing, I should be so lucky." The Jews call it doing shtick. "Oy Vey" the guy was really good at it.

His corporation never paid any dividends, the stock was never issued, but it was authorized. Little did I know that most of the people I ran into in Utah had the same deal. Everybody had a corporation with their father, brother, sister, and mother as shareholders. Everybody traded corporate papers among themselves and claimed they were just as good as money. I think I bought into all of them at one time or another. Bob Redford joked at the Utah Bankers' convention, "Utah is where the money flows in and never leaves the valley again." He got away with it because he brought millions into the valley and he was married to a good Mormon girl, but they sure weren't happy that he said it out loud, especially after they had just extended him a ten million dollar line of revolving credit. The bankers later forgave his inadvertent mistaken transgression because he shared the wealth with them.

In the mid nineteen seventies a seven foot one inch giant moved to Utah. He moved from Los Angeles' because the cops cracked down on the Hells Angels motorcycle gang. The angels were into the drug business big time. You might say they unionized their efforts. It became so blatant that the cops had to quit stealing the drugs back out of the evidence room and returning it for a piece of the action. California's Chief Parker cleaned up L.A. It got too hot for them in Los Angeles. I don't know why the Hells Angels decided on Utah as their new home.

Maybe all those Mormon Angels on the top of their temples made Dave and his gang think they would welcome them with open arms and be receptive to an incursion by outside angels. Whatever it was, it didn't work. One hundred and ten Hells Angels roaring into Lehi, Utah on Harley Davidson motorcycles didn't exactly make the welcome wagon roll out.

I don't think Dave deciding to call himself "The Holy Ghost" helped much either. When they bought a local church building for sixty five thousand dollars in hard-earned drug money, it further raised local peoples' suspicions. I think it was when they ripped the pews out of the church building that they bought and threw them on the front lawn that got some people hot. I believe the rest tipped over the edge into open resentment when Dave, The Holy Ghost Longo, imported whores and started selling drugs openly on the streets and at the schoolyard. To make it a little more interesting and in keeping with Dave's low profile approach to things, his gang donned karate gi's and blocked the only intersection with a light in town every day at high noon. Too bad Gary Cooper didn't see that. They did kata! Which some of my readers may know is a highly stylized and sometimes noisy exercise. It brought the house down. Locally people thought the denizens of hell, real demons, had come to possess their small town. They had that part right.

I got a call from a high ranking Mormon official that in no uncertain terms wanted me to go to Dave, ask him to leave Utah, get his response, and report back to him. Like any sane person would do I asked, "Why Me?"

His response was, "Because your name has come up before us." That worried me a lot. I tried to get him to agree to take my name off whatever list they were working from but he was non-committal about that.

I decided to go fishing. I am an avid fisherman. I fish for trophy size trout with ultra light equipment. That means a two-dollar reel and a two-dollar pole I bought by mail out of the Sunday newspaper. I threw my Kung Fu gi in the back of my souped up Volkswagen, just for emergencies. My car was tricked out with a Porsche engine, water alcohol injection, turbocharged etc., just in case I had to beat a hasty retreat. The German Brown trout were spawning in the Fremont River. The gi was only if I couldn't out think the bad guys. Smart people stay alive by picking their fights. Never let the other guy pick for you.

I collected three small boys for protection from a friend of mine and headed out to the Fremont River in Southern Utah. We just coincidentally had to pass through Lehi, Utah at high noon where Dave and his boys were holding the town hostage. When we drove into town I had not disclosed to my passengers anything about my ancillary interest in the town.

Two cop cars were on both sides of the street with lights flashing, but they were just parked as observers they told me. I didn't disturb them except to tell them I was just passing through and I needed to talk to the big guy in the middle of the street. They thought I was crazy, but let me do it. One cop said, "It's your funeral, help yourself."

I was five foot ten inches tall and weighed one hundred sixty pounds. I was dressed in jeans and a sweatshirt. I was not very imposing. But I did get the head angels attention when I walked from the cop car over to the middle of the street and asked to talk to him. I was longing for a sling and some smooth stones right then. A staff would have been nice. Even a suit of armor and a horse would have been welcome.

Dave started screaming, "What do you think you're doing? Can't you see I'm doing something? Do you want to die here and now?"

I told him, "No, but I want you to leave Utah and go back to L.A."

He went nuts, "I oughta kill you right now, why should I leave Utah? I like it here; I'm never leaving Utah."

I then told him about the legend of the destroying angel that protected the valley from evil, that no evil that came into the valley could remain there for long because God would send his destroying angel, the same one that killed the first born of Egypt when an evil Pharaoh wouldn't let the Israelites go free to worship God.

He laughed and said, "I am the destroying angel and because you have angered me, you have to fight me to the death.

I explained that he was too big for me to fight.   I was too little and death was too permanent. It seemed real final to me. I asked how much he weighed?

He proudly told me, "Three hundred thirty six pounds."

I then offered him a counter proposal. I would fight him, but not to the death. If I won, he left the valley and took his people with him. He agreed, but only after he turned around and winked at his men and they all laughed.

Then he tried to make me a very generous offer. He told me that he would take my wife and turn her into a real woman, and keep my children alive as his personal pets. He shouldn't have said that because it raised the stakes a little and got me centered and completely focused.   Then I tried to tell him he didn't want my wife, that she could be a complete troll and that she wasn't woman enough for him. I explained that my kids would make real lousy pets because they didn't always obey very well.   Besides that, my neighbors had much cuter kids that he might like better than mine.

He didn't want to hear it so it became show and tell time. It turned out that King David was right! One person and God can make a majority. Dave got too angry. He over committed himself and went out of control. He charged me with a loud yell that shook the ground. I stepped aside and kicked his kneecap off. When he fell I kicked him in the temple. Not too hard because I didn't want to accidentally kill him. I needed him conscious so he could verify our contract. I pushed him on his back and explained that he and I had to agree to some common realities together. I placed one foot on his Adams Apple also known as the larynx. Over this organ there is a protective hyoid cartilage. I explained to him it takes eighteen ounces of pressure to split the hyoid cartilage. It looks like a wishbone. If I do that it will pierce both of your carotid arteries.

"Do you still want to fight to the death with me?" Personal pain can be most instructive.

Since I was standing on his neck he could only mutter a guttural response that sounded a lot like No. I further instructed him he had to keep his word and leave the Salt Lake Valley and not come back. He agreed to all the above caveats that our contract contained. I let him up and helped him to his feet after I slid his Patella (kneecap) back into place.

He kept his word and left, but not until he shouted, "I better never see you again because I'll be packin and I'll shoot you dead."

I retorted, "Yeah! Yeah! Pharaoh said that to Moses but things didn't turn out that way."

He yelled as I went to my car, "Well you ain't Moses.

I couldn't resist with, "And you aren't Pharaoh." I reported back to my uplink.

Well, the boys and I went fishing and caught full stringers of fish and I thanked God for not letting me die in the streets of Lehi, Utah. I didn't feel comfortable with anyone else driving my car anyway, but he knew that. Any time you think your problems are solved and all the major misadventures that are destined to befall you have occurred, fate just loves to step in and deal you a new hand. I've learned it's not the cards that you are dealt, but how you play the hand you are dealt that keeps the game interesting.

Two years later Dave Longo returned to Utah. Only this time he came alone without his gang. He set up shop within six blocks of the Mormon temple in downtown Salt Lake City. The Mormons were incensed and deeply offended. He was ensconced in the penthouse of the Royal Inn Hotel.

I received the call again, only this time it was a little bit louder and a little bit worse. I went to visit Dave. When I got to the Royal Inn hotel it was snowing those big flakes the size of a silver dollar that can cover your car in an hour. I hit the button on the speaker box and a woman answered. I gave her my name and told her I needed to see Dave. She yelled to him; he was out on the roof making snowballs and throwing them at moving cars in the street.

He told her, "Let him come on up; he knows what to expect."

When I got out of the elevator, I was in their front room. A woman stoned out of her mind and a bunch of mean looking rag tag kids all drugged into oblivion were sitting on a beautiful couch they had broken the legs off. They were watching Freddy Kruger on T.V. Dave motioned to me to join him on the roof. I did so. I saw the light flicker in his eyes and I knew instantly that he intended to throw me off the roof.

I said, "Don't even think about it, Dave."

"What's that?" he asked blank faced with his most innocent voice.

"What you're thinking of doing. If you succeed someone much more terrible then me will come, that I assure you, you don't want to meet."

He laughed and said, "I'm back and I ain't ever leaving Utah again, not for you, the army, the navy, the marines, or the Mormons. You know what? He was right.

I left that night. The next morning the newspapers had huge headlines screaming from the front page. It seems a being at least eight feet tall visited them and threw the entire Longo family out into the street twelve floors down. This was no small feat considering there was a forty-foot set back from the curb. When I called the brethren, I asked them if they had seen the morning papers. They said that they had, but they didn't seem surprised by it. When I asked if they had any comment on the news they only had one thing to say, "God will not be mocked."

Only one member of the Longo family survived, Cindy is now a hopeless cripple living in a wheelchair in Spokane, Washington. She isn't giving any interviews and doesn't want to talk about it.

My advice to all my readers is if you are ever hopelessly outnumbered by countless foes,

"Keep the Faith! Unseen help may arrive just in the nick of time." (smile).

SUCCESS

Leonard Bokelman was a big German with eyes as cold as ice. I first met him in a Denny's restaurant in Northgate, a suburb of Seattle. He was with a little redheaded guy he called Red. Red had called me on the phone and said he and Leonard Bokelman wanted to meet me in a public place somewhere in Seattle. I was used to paranoid people so it didn't set off any alarm bells in my brain. Since I didn't know either guy, I asked, "Who gave you my name? And what do you want me for?"

Sometimes, Greenwood detective agency used me to transport money to the bank, or escort someone in safety. I occasionally did body guard work for them and others. But, I always like to know who I'm working for and what the detail is before I commit myself.

One time not too long ago a detective agency asked me to work a detail for them. It should have been a simple assignment. I got to choose between escorting a businessman to the bank to make a deposit on Saturday, or running security at a wedding. I chose the businessman because I wouldn't have to wear a necktie. I'm a real deep guy, a real heavy thinker as you can tell by the aforementioned. I'll work just about any caper I don't have to wear a necktie for. Someone once told me, "You don't like neckties because you don't have a neck."

I wasn't offended by their comment. I just explained to them that only sissies have necks.

The owners of the detective agency worked the wedding security detail themselves. They got shot in the hand because one guy on the detail let the jilted ex-lover into the wedding. He had been given a photo of the bad guy, but it had him with a beard in street clothes. And the new guy didn't recognize him without a beard in a suit.

I guess when the minister asked the telling question, "If anyone here as an objection to these two people being wed let them speak now, or forever hold their peace..." The jilted dude must have thought he said, "Let them rest in peace" because he opened fire immediately. I visited the owner of the agency in the hospital with her hand all bandaged up. It was hard to keep a straight face when she told me what happened.

Leonard and Red told me they had a business deal for me. That usually means some guy with no assets and no references wants to borrow a million dollars or more on nothing but their good word, telling me what fine people they are, and they never lie, or like the guy who called me from a bar at three o'clock a.m. from Cheyenne, Wyoming to tell me had an idea for a revolutionary new beer can opener and he just needed a few million dollars to develop it. Of course I got out of bed, addressed an envelope and sent it to him right away. I expect people to occasionally act stupid, but if you let them, some people want to abuse the privilege.

I met Leonard and Red at Denny's at the appointed time. They were casting furtive glances around the room and acting like they expected the cops to bust in at any time. We introduced ourselves to each other and they asked the waitress for a private table. I liked her response. "All our tables are private," she said. We seated ourselves and Leonard placed his briefcase on the seat between us. He had been hugging the briefcase like it had the elixir of life, or the only antidote for a rare poison. I'm used to people giving me a long narrative, or big preamble before they launch into the meat of what it is they want the money for.

So, when Leonard threw thirty-three million dollars worth of emeralds on the table and asked, "How much can I borrow against these babies if I use them for collateral?" I was a little taken aback. I asked him to put them away; we were attracting too much attention.

My mental computer went into high-speed overdrive. "What do you want the money for if you have these?" I ingeniously asked.

"I want to buy an interest in an oil well being drilled in Deuschane, Utah," he answered.

You could have swept me away with a feather. I knew the area and some people that worked the Deuschane Roosevelt area of Utah. It's the entrance way to Flaming Gorge, Utah. A friend and I had spent several summers floating the Green river fishing for trophy trout there. I knew they had oil there from producing wells, and some of them did quite well.

I tried to disabuse these guys of having any hope. I explained that I didn't know anyone to make that kind of loan, and that the chance of the well he was interested in, coming into oil was like a billion to one odds against it. I told them seven hundred fifty thousand dollars was impossible. The emeralds weren't cut or polished yet, and as unfinished material they might as well be in the ground, or still in the riverbed, or the magnate they retrieved them from.

Then it hit me; I knew where I had seen Leonard Bokelman. I never forget a face. All you do is memorize their eyes, no matter what happens to the rest of their features. They can't change their eyes. Ralph Waldo Emerson said, "The eyes are the window to the soul," that is, if they have a soul.

There is something about people who murder. Their eyes change; it's like looking into the eye of a great white shark. They would not feel anything at all while they engulfed you. They have no feeling whatsoever. Killing you or letting you live is just the flip of a coin. It could go either way depending on the luck of the draw. You have to convince a murderer there is something to be gained by letting you live.

In the words of an Australian, who was recently arrested for chumming great white sharks with bloody chunks of horsemeat off Bondi Beach, Australia, he said he did it so his friends could videotape him patting them on the snouts when they came rushing in to take a big bite of the bloody carcass. The harbor cops were appalled at his audacity when he told them it's okay as long as you stay away from their bitey parts. Now there is a day's work to make you think.

My mental computer kicked into high gear again as I exclaimed, "These aren't your emeralds. They belonged to a little guy named Scotty that wore a Puka shell necklace that I saw you with fifteen years ago in the Oregon First National bank building in Portland, Oregon." Scotty was killed in Guatemala during a raid in a Cantina by the solideros, a death squad, I read about it in time magazine seven years ago.

"Well they are mine now," was all Leonard volunteered. I told them that I couldn't help them. I paid the check and left.

I heard from Leonard and Red for the next six weeks until I was going nuts. Every time I answered the phone it seemed like they were on it. They either were stalking me, or they were psychic. I couldn't seem to avoid them or get clear of them.

Imagine my surprise when I answered the door one day just as this beautiful well-dressed woman was about to knock on the door. We both stammered for a second as I told her I was just leaving. She handed me an invitation to a very exclusive Christmas party at a major hotel. She said her name was Melinda and that she was just dropping off the invitations for Leonard. I thought I must have heard her wrong. She was a real class act. What would she be doing with one of the S.S. Gestapo boys I wondered.

Well I went to the soirée and it was first class all the way. I had worn my back up suit instead of the good one. It got me in the door, but just barely. The last time I saw anything like this party was at the Ritz Carlton Hotel in Boston, Massachusetts where I was doing some business with Boston First National bank for one of their clients. I was very impressed to say the least. Melinda hung on my arm like she belonged there. I wasn't in any hurry to shake her off either. I figured she was the only reason they didn't ask me to leave. I had on my cheap suit, my gold ring with the cubic zirconium, and my knock off Rolex watch, so I didn't look like a total swine at a pearl party, but I definitely felt out of place.

They even served canapés of stuffed crab and oysters Rockefeller while we were waiting for the dinner. Melinda guided me through the meal with style and grace.

When the time came for the obligatory after dinner speaker to say a few words, I thought, this is it. This is where I have to earn the dinner I just ate. Instead Leonard got up and proposed a toast. Melinda had filled my glass with grape juice, so I would fit right in with the rest of the winebibbers. Leonard's toast was unforgettable. He had raised the seven hundred fifty thousand dollars. He and Red had bought into the oil well in Deuschane, Utah. The well had come in like gangbusters. It was pumping thirty- three hundred barrels a day. Blimey, I was blown away. It never felt so good being so wrong. I ended up apologizing to everybody. Nobody guesses right all the time. That's what makes life a crapshoot, even on a good day.

THE GREEN RIVER EPISODE

Melvin Foster was a taxicab driver. He drove cab for Far West Cab Company. Far West Cab Company is the largest taxicab company in Seattle, Washington. That doesn't necessarily mean they are the best cab company, just the company with the most cabs, and the most drivers on the road.

I saw Melvin in his parked cab outside the Greyhound bus station 4 or 5 days a week, usually in the late afternoon, or late at night. He was a street person that was one cab ride away from being homeless. He liked the night action. Now cab drivers in general are not well liked by the United States government. They do all their business in cash, and if there is a cab driver that never skimmed, shorted, or worked without dropping the flag I never met them.

It is an industry that is rife with fraud, lies, and misrepresentations. From the top down, or the bottom up if you care to figure it in either direction. I've heard the Government does not like whores, or drug dealers for the same reason. It's hard to fix what their true income is and how much of that income is taxable. In addition to trying to get the fox to incriminate himself when he is self-appointed to guard the hen house, it is hard to know if the fox traded goods for his, or her services.

Now Melvin had appetites that differed from just the ordinary cab drivers' appetites. He discovered chicken meat children that roam the streets get tired. The bus station won't let them crash inside, or take up permanent residence, let alone panhandle change inside, or outside the bus station. Runaway children have no sense of yesterday, let alone tomorrow. There is only the now moment that they live in. They know that the rule of the curb is there is no tomorrow, if you have money, spend it now. So, the Greyhound station saw plenty of action. There were video games, rest rooms, wall lockers, and Burger King attached to the terminal proper.

Seattle rains sometimes. You may have heard that somewhere before. Usually it is just overcast and drizzles, but even so, it cools off at night. Kids are afraid to sleep in doorways. You usually get mugged, jacked, or charged as they say it on the street. Since the bus station is downtown in the belly of the beast, there are cops around, but when something goes down, it is over so fast that the cops don't have time to put their donuts down. That is part of the appeal of life on the street. I've attempted rescue efforts before and the axiom you can take the kid out of the street, but you can't take the street out of the kid once they've gotten used to living life on the run is only too true. They seem to always go back to easy choices. Like do I do the drug, drink the drink, rob the guy, or not? Anything else in the straight world has too many rules. Not everybody that is homeless is that way because they have to be. Some people don't like rules. So they jump over the fence to the other side and live outside the rules. But—I'm here to tell you when a kid under twelve years of age makes that decision, it has some real dangers that even watching endless television doesn't prepare them for.

Melvin was one of those dangers. He would let you take a nap in the back seat of his cab. If you had drugs, he might trade you. If you had enough drugs, he'd jack you for them. If you didn't have any other commodity to bargain with, it was all about your body. How badly did you need sleep? Enough to let Melvin have sex with you? Traditional sex, or otherwise, he didn't care. But you had to be careful because depending what drugs or alcohol Melvin had consumed previously determined whether he violated your body minimally, or whether he sold you to some other deviant vermin that would pay his price. Even at its very best, no optimal deal ever struck rewarded the kid enough to make them flee the scene, or never take another chance. I was drawn into this degrading picture by an emergency telephone call to my work. The word on the curb was you could call me if it's an emergency at my work. He is mobile and he will find you and get to you the same day. But there may be some delay in getting to you, depending on how far away he is from you. If they called at home, I always went right away. The call about Melvin came to my secretary at work. She recognized the fear in the kids voice and hooked us up immediately. Now the owners of National Sign were observant enough to know that I sometimes hurriedly set my work aside to go rescue a street kid. They neither encouraged nor discouraged it. It didn't happen very often, once or twice a month. I was generally very zealous not to compromise my employer's time, interest or money. I made a special effort to over compensate any time with an extra abundance of free time. This kept the playing field level for everybody, and it kept me gainfully employed. (smile)

The caller said, "Come quick, somebody slipped Angel a bad load. She is trying to walk out of an upstairs window of the Westin hotel. Get over here quick."

Angel was an 11-year-old girl I had met once before that ran the mean streets of Seattle. She had been living off of dempsey dumpster diving. The kids use a pay phone near a Dempsey dumpster, usually near an alley. They call in a bogus fast food delivery order, pizza most of the time. When the driver makes the so-called delivery. There is no one there by that name. Nobody ordered a Pizza so the driver tosses it in the dumpster. As soon as he drives off, it's chow time.

Angel tried waiting in the dumpster to get a few extra slices before someone bigger and meaner got it all. That was a big mistake. Somebody locked the dumpster and she was scheduled for pick up when I arrived and let her out. But a bad load meant someone put some arsenic in with the LSD or they angel dusted her. Either way, she was a goner unless someone cooled her out quickly. I got to the Westin Hotel, went upstairs and got things back under control. I found out quickly that Melvin Foster had beaten her up, and then raped her in the back seat of his cab. He then beat her up some more with a hot load of drugs to shut her up.

I decided it was time to pay Melvin Foster a little visit. When I got to him he was waiting cab turn at the curb outside the bus depot. Since I was still dressed in the white man's business uniform, a suit, shirt and a tie, I got into his cab like any other fare…When he slid behind the wheel I grabbed him by his long greasy hair and snatched his head backward over the seat. I then pinched his Adams apple so he couldn't cry out. I whispered in his ear, "Don't try to talk. You can't anyway. Just listen; with eighteen ounces of pressure I can crush your voice box completely. You will never talk again. With twenty-two ounces of pressure I can crush your trachea. You will not live long enough to get help. You need to get yourself treated. You gave syphilis to my friend, Angel. You raped her and tried to kill her. You gave syphilis to a ten-year-old boy in the back of your cab. I don't like you. I want to hurt you more than you have ever been hurt before. I'll give you two days to make an appointment to get yourself treated. If you don't, I will send someone that is truly terrible. They will hurt you a lot more than I'm hurting you now." Do we agree on this?

I loosened the hold on his hair enough for him to feebly nod yes. He lied! I left thinking we had an understanding. He didn't get himself treated; instead, he tried to terrorize the street kids. His avowed goal was to infect as many kids as possible before his disease got too painful and messy to keep driving cab.

I called a favor due me from some people in Chinatown. After a few weeks he let his guard down. Three weeks later he answered a midnight run to the airport. When he got the bell from the dispatcher, it was a legitimate call. When the three men got in his cab, he smelled money. Chang told me later that he was looking at them in the mirror when Chang reached over the seat and cut off Melvin's ear with a straight razor. He flipped his sliced ear up on the dash and said, "Get your self fixed," as they all got out of his cab and calmly walked away.

Melvin must have panicked because they had him on the 6:00 o'clock news the next night with a bloody bandage on one side of his head. He had turned himself into the police as the green river killer. It was unbelievable to the police and it was very unbelievable to me. He later got sentenced to three years in Walla Walla penitentiary. The cops knew he didn't have the stones to be the green river killer, but he was punished anyway for trifling with the system. A lot of kids had a big party in downtown Seattle that night.

CHILD SUPPORT

My new wife and I got into a disagreement. She had three kids when I met her. We dated off and on for four years. She had another guy, a doctor she liked. I was surprised she even gave me a tumble, being as how I was a convicted felon, a.k.a. a social leper. When the system spits you back out into the public domain, you might as well ring a silver bell like the lepers do in India. They ring a bell and yell, "Leper, unclean, coming through." Boy, do the people scatter. If you don't move, they shove their diseased limbs in your face and you get a zoom lens close up of what could happen to you and you quickly move for them.

I had a few bucks. Linda, my new wife knew I had it because I had just sold my car. She had been fronting me a place to live, providing food, etc. I agreed to pay her. But I didn't know that my ex-wife could reach out her long bony claw from Idaho to Washington and demand eighty four thousand dollars for past child support while I was in prison. When she divorced me, I gave her everything I owned, because she perceived the prison experience would kill me. Plus, I didn't need possessions in hell. When I didn't die, it was a big disappointment for some people. Washington State had a lesbian child support officer who loved to hurt men. She had several "I want to hurt men elves" that worked for the state and did her constant bidding. I'm surprised the state had to pay them at all. I do believe they love their jobs, and would work for nothing other than the satisfaction of hurting a man, any man, that the state would let them.

Every year the State of Washington prints in the newspapers how many men it has ground up into pixie dust and how much loot they collected. It's millions and millions of dollars. My wife thought I had exaggerated the prosecutor's sexual orientation until she went to court with me one day dressed in shorts because it was summer time. When the afore mentioned prosecutor put her hand on my wife's bare thigh and asked her in a very friendly way, "Is there anything I can do for you sweetie?"

My wife pointed to me and told her she was with me. She recoiled like a rattlesnake bit her hand. I laughed out loud at my wife's consternation. She thought I had categorized her as queer or a dyke out of anger at my personal circumstances. She found out I don't hang false jackets on people.

Most people don't know that Child Support Enforcement is a for profit entity. It takes thirty percent of everything it collects off the top, up front. It also charges twelve percent interest on the principle of the unpaid balance on each and every account. It forces the court and its officers to do their job, no exceptions and no circumstances to the contrary. Now I know the world is full of deadbeat dads. I believe it is in the best interest of the children and society for the dad to pay so the state and Federal Government doesn't have to pay. However, I think it should be disclosed that a judgment is ordered against the dad with no mitigating circumstances. My ex wife was earning forty seven thousand dollars per year and had a paid for house, two new cars and was not dependent upon the state. She just wanted to hurt me. It worked real good.

Senator Patrick Monihan predicted when he got the welfare system into play years ago that it would become too cumbersome, that too many minority teen age girls would get pregnant and plug the system up with unwanted children. Nobody believed him then, but they sowed the wind and now they are reaping the whirlwind. They believe him now. I was ordered to go to court and pay three hundred dollars by Friday. If I didn't pay, I went to jail.

My new wife wanted the three hundred dollars I held out from her on the sale of my car. I told her, "No!" I had just given her thirteen hundred dollars and I wouldn't give any more at that time, she'd have to wait.

Her response was, "Pay up, or get out."

So I got out. I got as far away from Seattle as possible. I rode the old loping dog bus to South Carolina and got a job transporting abused kids to safe houses. It didn't pay much, but it was honest work, and it made me feel good about myself.

One day the phone rang for me. It was my wife Linda. She knocked me off my feet with the news she gave me. She had joined the Mormon Church and wanted me back. She explained that when I married her two of her, daughters were whacked out of the pocket. They were labeled retarded. One was institutionalized for life. The other operated between the ages of a three to seven year old. The Mormons gave a blessing to the semi-normal one. She was grand mal epileptic up to twenty seizures a day. Her seizures stopped and went away. I went home to my new wife and daughter. They had become latter day saints. I was still a latter day aint. Boy, what a switcharoo that was. It took me some little time to adjust to it.

MR. MONEYBAGS

Everyone knows that the Mormons don't have a paid ministry. They have a lay membership. The ecclesiastical authority over eight to twelve hundred members is called a Bishop. He has a full time job aside from his church duties. I went to church with my family one day and a high ranking high priest pulled me aside in the hall and asked me if I wanted to buy a house with nothing down, no interest and no assets necessary. It didn't matter that I had been in prison. I thought I had died and gone to hog heaven. He handed me a slip of paper with a 1-800 number on it. So I called the number and the people were cheerful and happy to make my acquaintance, too cheerful I thought.

Elliot Janeway the British economist has pointed out quite rightly, I believe, that the two most expensive purchases made by the average citizen are a house and a car, in that order unless they invest in a business. The average American will never have, more than twenty thousand dollars cash at once in their lifetime, independent of a home interest.

So I was very interested in being able to qualify for a home for my new family. I've ridden some pretty hairy roller coasters in my life, but the one I climbed onto with my wife and Robert Darnell proved to be the scariest ride of all times. We went to a meeting in a rented hall. Everyone had to have picture I.D. You signed a list that had indescribable punishments if you told what you saw and heard in their meeting. It also had unbelievable rewards for getting in on the ground floor.

A guy got up and welcomed everyone and told amazing facts and figures about the economy and the costs of living etc. He promised to introduce us to a guy that had more gold than Fort Knox. This guy had a personal pipeline to the United States Mint. He could personally with his unlimited resources, cash, real estate, and credit issue a MasterCard to everyone in the room and let us find, our dream house. Mr. Moneybags was going to buy us all a new house. I looked around the room and saw pimps, dope dealers, welfare moms, and myself and thought isn't that wonderful. The losers of the world are all going to get a new house tonight.

Well, the first two hours were spent telling us how unfair the credit system is; that the rich have most of the money and that living rich is better than living poor. By the time several overly enthusiastic pitchmen and women finished with us, I was on cloud nine. Everybody in the room looked like they were on Prozac or Paxil. I couldn't get out of that room fast enough to get my ten new recruits. The next two hours brought us back down to earth. The complex formula for creating wealth was secret and mysterious. As closely as I could tell, we were going to spend ourselves rich. The more we spent the more money that poured into us. I was going to buy the world and share it with everybody. Mr. Moneybags had the job of financing everybody.

We found out we all got to have new cars, yachts, jet stream airplanes or anything else we wanted. Aladdin and his magic lamp were our very own for the rubbing. Aye, "there's the rub," as Shakespeare intoned in my ear. Like ants rushing out to a picnic, we all stormed out of that room; our dreams got bigger and bigger. Realtors in town were all eager to make our acquaintance. Especially, when we told them that the house we would be buying would be paid for with cash. We looked at houses until our eyes fell out of our heads. We had shifted to palaces and whole kingdoms with servants and everything. We were lowering the drawbridge to good times and heaven on earth.

But those realtors are a shifty lot. They make you list what you already own before they will sell you anything else. They won't even take their feet off their rented desks if you don't reek of wealth already. We reeked but it wasn't from wealth. We took our paperwork to Mr. Moneybags. He stamped it approved. We had our ten new guys already signed up. We were moving on up to the Eastside. We were getting ready to call the movers and everything when a glitch slowly appeared. Mr. Moneybags, because of some personal credo he assumed for himself, limited himself to how many millions of dollars he would spend per day. He didn't want to attract too much attention to himself because due to the jealousy and envy of others, he could topple the entire American economy, maybe even the whole worlds economy. We went ahead with our plans. We were going to buy a new home for everyone we knew. We might even buy some for people we didn't know, just because it felt so good to share with others. We were going to free the slaves, and buy new homes for all the orphan children of the world. Since the more we spent with this new complex mysterious formula of Mr. Moneybags, the more new money it created. The sky was the limit. We were sure that as soon as all the people on earth had a new home, Jesus was coming back to earth to live with us.

I was excited. My wife had visions of eliminating poverty in our lifetime. No one was ever going to be poor again. We had a new cause; we were soldiers in a war on poverty. BAM: It all ended suddenly. On the evening news they were hooking up Mr. Moneybags. They arrested our dreams come true guy. He was some twit living in a cheap apartment in Tacoma named Robert Darnell. He didn't have a pot to piss in, or a window to throw it out of. We were undone.

It seems Mr. Moneybags had fabulous visions when he didn't take his medication. As any Manic Depressive can tell you without the help of Lithium Carbonate, they believe they can do anything. The sky really is the limit. So my advice to anyone dealing with hucksters is to check their Medical profile before you buy into anything they want you to do.

In Mexico they have a saying when somebody goes crazy. They say, "They have gone south for awhile. They will be back later." It lets everybody off the hook, nobody feels guilty, and when they return to reality, you can welcome them back.

The Quakers have a saying, "All the world is mad except for me and thee, and sometimes I have doubts about thee" This too, defuses what can be an ugly entanglement.

I have a friend whose dad was an engineer in Richland, Washington. The engineer went mad as a hatter. He started remodeling their West Seattle Home at three o'clock in the morning. Nobody thought too much of it until he tried to remodel the neighbors' houses in the wee hours of the morning, picked all their flowers and brought them home and laid them on the doorstep that was his alter of devotion to his beloved wife.

We received a letter from Mr. Moneybags a few months later. It was a very poor photocopy. The inmates in prison don't have access to high quality copy machines, because if they did, they might try to make money with them. And- I don't mean earn money with them. They would make money with them. It's their thing if you know what I mean. Mr. Moneybags sent us a "WHAT IF LETTER". It was a bunch of loosely strung words that all asked, "WHAT IF?" The last sentence was, "What if you loaned me a few hundred dollars for my defense, and what if I didn't pay it back?" We didn't answer the letter because we figured he must be off his Lithium again. They say it seriously interferes with people drinking alcohol.

Well, we didn't get our dream home, but we got an education instead. Some of you might have had similar experiences in your life, if not, then you just haven't been trying hard enough. I always liked the sobriquet of Roy Rogers the singing cowboy. "Happy trails to you."

Incidentally, Roy Rogers tried to sell me real estate in the desert in California. He even called it happy valley. We were eating chicken at his ranch. He was presiding. Dale Evans was by his side when they closed the corral on us yahoos. They were selling Ranchetts to everyone that would buy one. I looked up at Trigger, the wonder horse, that was stuffed standing behind us and looked at Dale Evans across the table and wondered aloud if he was going to have her stuffed, too. It kinda wore out my welcome. They sort of closed me out of the opportunity of a lifetime. So be careful going through life. Life is a minefield if you can get to the end of it without losing your arms and legs, you have done real well.

CHARITY

My wife Linda was very unhappy and it was starting to affect me adversely. There is a saying in the world and on the curb of life, "If your wife is unhappy, chances are real good you probably will be unhappy, too."

I usually am the first to arise; I'm an early riser because that is the quiet time of the day for meditation and reflection. It gives you a chance to get centered so the world doesn't push you off center so easily. It prevents road rage and every other type of malady our high-pressure society suffers from.

My wife, on the other hand rolls, out of bed does four cups of coffee and a half a pack of cigarettes and hits the ground running. I noticed the disturbed sleep pattern and knew we were both in for a bout of depression. Depression to my mind is the most undiagnosed malady of our generation. I believe it is due to false expectations that we hold onto for ourselves. You almost have to let the person slide down to a certain level before they are even approachable about the subject. If you move too soon they go into denial and it becomes untreatable.

I found her sitting at the kitchen table staring into space with her head leaning on her hand. I greeted her with, "What's wrong with you?" I was never a candidate for our diplomatic core. She broke into tears. Tears are always a little unnerving, but I knew in my heart of hearts that people cry for themselves in spite of what they say to the contrary. Since I had never seen her cry before, I thought I had hit a nerve of some kind. I let her cry herself out. She was unhappy with herself and her life.

She had two retarded daughters and one that had distanced herself. She was a good worker, but only worked to get a paycheck to pay her bills. She was falling behind and felt like a failure. I told her it was the American way. Everybody wrestled demons of a similar nature. The British call it the curse of the working class. It goes with the territory we carve out for ourselves. That didn't placate or reassure her very much.

So I moved on with, "What would you like to do if money were no object?" It's hard to get people to change gears when they have tunnel vision. She decided she would like to help children. My wife's birth sign is the crab. Crabs are hard on the outside but soft on the inside. That fits her perfectly. The journey of a thousand miles begins with the first step. So we took the first step. We went down to the Federal Building and picked up the forms to form a 501 (c)(3) tax-free charity.

She named it *"The Children's Foundation."* Their mission statement was tightly focused. It was to provide Christmas for every institutionalized child in Washington State. The paper work was daunting. She kept throwing it away in disgust. I kept retrieving it from the garbage and putting it away for awhile until she was ready to do a few more pages. I'm not stubborn, but my ex wife used to tell me if I drowned she was looking for my body upstream. Eventually every question was answered and the application was complete. Oh happy day! The fees were paid and the application was submitted appropriately. On Christmas Eve day it was approved.

Then the real work began. We both worked full time and cared for our children. Any time we didn't work went into collecting presents, soliciting volunteer help, and getting the names and locations of all the children that needed help. We ended up with more than twenty five hundred children that had no Christmas planned for them. We got every child the gift they wanted.

Then David Horne the assistant Attorney General subpoenaed us with sworn affidavits at his office downtown. We were both scared, but puzzled. When we appeared, we were taken into separate rooms and sworn in under oath and told everything you say can and will be used against you in a court of law. I had a premonition some time before and had my name removed from the board of the charity. I perceived somebody would try to impugn the charity for having an ex-felon on the board. It proved to be more than prophetic.

A yuppie girl we had employed tried to rip off money and toys from the kids. We fired her immediately. I wasn't diplomatic about it. I told her anybody that would stoop so low as to rob vulnerable kids doesn't deserve to live in my book. Get your shit and get out. Go rob somebody else. She turned us in to the D.A. as a get back. I found out it was no longer politically correct to do what I did. David Horne proceeded to intimidate us and inform us that he didn't believe in charities. He stated he wouldn't have any charities in the state if it were up to him. He perceived they were all a ploy, a rip off and a ruse for people to steal money. None of them were real in his opinion. "Besides," he said, retarded kids don't know what Christmas is anyway. He was supercilious and angry that we had lost sixteen thousand dollars of our own money to support this losing proposition. He then informed us he was going to put us out of business and use all the power at his disposal to close us down.

I explained to him that I was locked up with the baddest men on earth and he wasn't one of them, that it was our money we earned and spent, and retarded kids may not know what Christmas was, but they knew what kindness was.

Well, the rest is history. For five years we pushed a big rock up a very steep hill. We were harassed and audited and were required to constantly spend time making affidavits and reporting to David Horne who had ambitions to be in the Governors office.

But we finally lost. We shut our doors. He beat us to death. However, in that interim we learned many new things. We found out we were tougher than we thought we were and we adopted the mantra of Nietche "Any thing that doesn't kill you will make you stronger." No one can take from us the experience of getting, wrapping, and delivering 2500 Christmas presents to children who have no hope for anything, let alone for a better life or a tomorrow. We can only adjure everyone everywhere, if you have a dream to make the world a better place to live in, dream your dream, then wake up and make your dreams come true. It can happen to anybody that is willing to pay the price of their dream. The Chinese say the glory is not in never falling, but getting back up each time you fall and attempting again."

THE EPISODE OF ARIZONA REINSURANCE

Pat Lyons was a study in contradictions if there ever was one. He could be as unctuous as a minister giving last rites to a dying child and at the same time pick your pocket without you ever knowing you were relieved of the heavy burden of carrying excess cash you didn't really need. One of his employees described him as, "Slicker than greased owl shit on a glass doorknob." I personally admired his psychic ability to smell money. It didn't matter if it was hidden in the coat pocket of a religious congregation or secreted in some city's coffers. He could sense it, and find it unerringly like a homing missile attracted to body heat.

The guy was a financial terminator. I found out after several years of knowing him it was because he used to be a preacher of some merit in a small town in Washington. He successfully ran the church until the money got so huge he just had to relieve it of some of the extra cash that was burdening the church with sin and responsibility. It probably wouldn't have been noticed for a very long time, but concomitantly he began to counsel some of the sisters in the church. His personal attention knew no bounds until his wife began to constantly complain about the fact that he had time for everyone in the church except for her and their own children. Now this story is as old as Cain and Able. Wayward southern preachers are the grist of pulp fiction and early romance novels.

Pat was inexorably attracted to his brother's wife. She was a redhead and hotter than a firecracker if you know what I mean. She was not shy and did not do anything in a small way. It's a good thing Pat was a big man because she did him in a big way, too. It seems that there are limits even a small congregation can stand. Someone from the pulpit committee decided to look into the personal and financial affairs of the church. It was a nightmare for everybody. What followed was handled with as much discretion and civility as could be mustered under the circumstances, but it resembled the aftermath of a southern hurricane. I personally think it was when his brother got his gun and came looking for his wife late one night that tipped the frog into the milk pail. The rest was handled with circumspect decorum and quiet civility.

Pat moved from the area and took up residence in the tri-city area, Richland, Pasco, and Kennewick Washington. It was hundreds of miles from his wife and kids, his brother's wife and all the problems the church discovered it secretly had within. He then redrafted his resume and he was reborn as a city manager. In the next few years he conducted a symphony of largess and greed that went way beyond any imagination but his own.

The tri-city area started rolling in dough. It became a veritable flood of money. But after three years or so, someone took notice that tiny rivulets of cash were flowing elsewhere instead of

301

directly into the city's coffers. It was explained as cost overruns from mammoth fund raising efforts. The city decided after a quiet investigation that they did not have enough evidence to bring suit and have a very public trial without admitting their own stupidity in turning the town key over to a relative newcomer. So like an old fashioned town-taming cowboy, Pat decided to mount his horse and ride out of town. He was looking for a new town to tame. However, over the years his ever-escalating appetite for cash had burgeoned to where he decided to let it all hang out.

He rode into Seattle, Washington and discovered that the big money was moving to the eastside. Bellevue, Washington across lake Washington was a wealthy enclave and suburb of Seattle. It was the very place an entrepreneur of merit should rightly be ensconced. Like Julius Caesar riding into Rome after crossing the Rubicon, he decided that the phrase "Vini, Vini, Vicci, I came I saw, I conquered," was perfect for his next financial adventure.

This time he had a real lollapalooza in mind. It staggered more than one person's imagination. He met a handsome charismatic man named Ned. Some people say they met in a bar. While they were talking, Ned let slide that he could buy a re-insurance company for the paltry sum of fifteen thousand dollars. Normally this would have been too small an amount for Pat to be interested, but when he found out from Ned what a re-insurance company does and the amount of cash that it creates, the whole board room in his brain lit up. He was on fire with how he and Ned could both get very, very rich. He could sense the mother lode, the big bonanza lying just beyond the reach of their fingertips. They formed a company and the good times began to roll.

Now Ned had been a gunnery sergeant in Viet Nam and he knew how to stay cool under fire, but Viet Nam had left him with a serious predilection for liquor. He had a nice wife and some kids, and a secretary that loved him and would follow him into the mouth of hell if he asked her to. Ned treated his people well and he commanded their loyalty and respect. He was not mean spirited and calculating like Pat. He never suspected that Pat had a hidden agenda of relieving everybody of their cash, including Ned's.

Now a re-insurance company is an interesting entity. When an insurance company writes insurance on an individual they lay off their risk like a bookie does with horse racing. There is one subtle difference though. It is a highly regulated industry. It is controlled state by state by the insurance commissioner. When the risk pool is enlarged by a new premium being collected, only the actuarial amount of actually insuring the individual is kept. The rest has to be shared by the companies buying the rest of the unused portion of the premium. This is used for investment and financing purposes. That is how insurance companies build such magnificent ivory towers to themselves and their industry. They then become their own anchor tenants in a building that they finance the construction thereof! I liken it to lifting yourself up by your own bootstraps. It is an art when practiced properly, a real feat of legerdemain.

Well, Pat and Ned rented prestigious offices in a country park setting right off the main boulevard in Bellevue. Pat quickly swung his plan into action. If you delay sending the unused portion of the premium upstream for a while, nobody complains too much, at least not to the insurance commissioner. They make polite phone calls because they are used to it, taking some time for the business to be underwritten and booked. It's only when several months pass by that the complaints become more strident and threatening, or until an insured party needs a life saving operation.

When something catastrophic happens and it's life or death, you try to save your loved one at any cost. Pat's genius was that he specialized in writing policies on old people that couldn't buy coverage elsewhere, either because of age or pre-existing conditions that were unacceptable to other insurance agencies. He had a captive audience, but he also had a ticking time bomb. The bomb went off! Now Ned was a little naive to say the least. He turned the daily running of the business over to Pat. After all, the guy was a self-proclaimed *wunder kind* at finding new money and new people. They suddenly went from being small fry to big potatoes.

Ned only got into a brouhaha with Pat when an underpaid underling came to him with a raise request of five dollars per hour. The secretary was putting in sixty hours or more a week. She was on standby twenty-four hours a day, seven days a week. She reported and worked for four different bosses all making big dough. She wanted some crumbs to trickle down to her. The big bosses awarded themselves with salaries of twenty thousand dollars per month. And they all leased Van Plas Jaguars that cost in excess of fifty five thousand dollars each. When Pat refused her request for more money because she was a woman and was married she asked for an explanation. Pat studied her like a bug on the end of a pin. With cold detachment he told her "I never pay more than I have to for anybody or anything. I can replace you for less than I would have to pay you. Tell your husband to get a second job."

She suddenly saw daylight from out of the loyalty haze she was working under. She noticed things she never paid attention to before, like getting her paycheck and having to write a personal check back to the company as a tax write off. Pat had attracted a real estate company that was privately owned to log in with him. He had a private insurance agent that wrote business for them, a contractor that built houses, a retired black surgeon that raised money for their various financial dealings and enterprises, a famous sports figure that was honest and forthright, but was charmed into letting his name and persona be used to promote new investors. I tell you the guy had a silver tongue and could talk the birds of the air into coming down out of the trees and feeding out of his hand. However, one day a seismic tremor shook his overbuilt house of cards, and the entire edifice began to shake and tremble. Over a hundred people a day started calling to inquire about the status of their insurance. They discovered when they went into the hospitals for medical treatment that they didn't have any medical coverage. They couldn't understand it because they had paid their premiums to Arizona Re-insurance Company in good faith.

Well, the rest is history. The State of Arizona disavowed any responsibility. It seems there was not a lawful charter issued to sell insurance from there. Washington did not have any license to do so. Someone had forged the insurance commissioners signature and sold insurance without proper authorization. Pat hired temporary secretaries to answer the phones, and field the switchboard all day long. Angry upset people called dozens of times a day trying to unravel the Gordian knot.

Finally the insurance commissioner came with the U.S. Marshals and shut their doors permanently. Pat and Ned went to prison. I have no idea how many people may have died, nor do I know what the final curtain held for all the people tricked out of their money. I do know that somewhere in the world this story is playing out again. It probably just isn't being done on such a grand scale as this case was, or maybe it is, you might want to check your disclosure sheets on any polices that you are paying for. I know that I am checking mine for sure. (Smile)

TURNIPSEED

His name was Turnipseed, Ray Turnipseed. I met him at Lompoc Prison Camp. He was a quiet slightly built guy accompanied by a huge dude dressed in a conger eel leather coat. I didn't know they let guys have personal bodyguards in prison, but this guy had one. His name was Mac and he had a menacing air about him that made me not eager to talk to, or try to befriend him.

For the next two weeks I kept trying to avoid him. At the urging of others, I finally relented. I thought he might have wanted ladies to write to, or a writ of some kind. Other than the cops coming to me to start a corporation, those were usually the only reasons people I didn't know came to me unasked for.

I worked daily in the law library, the hospital, and the furniture shop. So I stayed busy. I put in twelve hour days to make the time pass more quickly, but I didn't ever solicit business. It came to me or I let it pass by. My fellow inmates, or constituents, were not the most reliable clientele anyone would want to be in bed with financially or any other way you might think of.

Finally Ray and Mac cornered me at the breakfast table and wanted to talk to me so, I let them lead me into a conversation. "What do you guys want?" I asked with my usual savoir-faire manner. I don't like to walk around the block to get next door.

Ray began by introducing me to Mac as his son and fall partner. This surprised me a little because I have stated heretofore the government doesn't like to let fall partners do time together. They have learned from sad experience that sometimes they get into additional mischief, like planning escapes together.

Ray it seems, all one hundred thirty five pounds of him with white hair, was a Puyallup Indian. Mac, who weighed in at three hundred seventy five plus, was an Indian too. The

Puyallup's were making around four million dollars a month. They were the second most prosperous Indian tribe in the United States. It seems Ray skimmed their casino proceeds before paying the taxes to Uncle Sam. His defense of they do it in Vegas wasn't quite good enough to get him off. The feds took the whole family to jail. Then to various prisons! Rays wife was doing time at Pleasanton Women's Prison in Pleasanton, California. Meanwhile Ray and Mac were doing time in Lompoc Prison Camp. I forget how many millions were involved, but it didn't matter because even though the state didn't make its case against them, it took them all away. The funny thing is they all received huge checks, sixteen thousand dollars apiece per month, while they were lounging in prison.

Ray wanted to offer me a job. I deferred for the moment because I didn't think it seemly to accept employment from a fellow inmate while incarcerated. At least I perceived the law would not like it even if it allowed it to be done. Well, I found Ray to be affable and funny. He and I played pool and talked about cabbages and kings, sealing wax and strings and other things, as Lewis Carrol would have intoned.

When I got out of prison and paroled to Seattle, I found one of my fellow inmates was being employed by Ray to deliver salmon to restaurants on the waterfront. I probably would have heard no more from them, but big Larry decided he could highjack his own truck load of salmon and not pay the people that fronted him the truck, the salmon, and the money he used to buy a used Volkswagen. I'm afraid greed has killed more deals than all the money in the world could have ever supplied.

The next thing I know Larry called me and told me his tale of woe and that I should use a secret knock whenever I came over to see him in his apartment in Bellevue. To make a long story short, I arranged a meeting with Ray and the boys and they agreed not to kill him. I guaranteed the return of their truck and some face-to-face time with Larry. Everybody was happy but Larry. I explained some fundamental truths to him. One: Kindness is not weakness. Two: he had to know his body was the collateral on the deal when he didn't sign anything, but took a forty thousand dollar truck on a handshake. Three: he needed to distance himself for a while and let things cool off, but not until after we had our conference.

I guaranteed him only safe passage for the conference. I told him the story of Longinus the Roman centurion who pierced the side of Jesus Christ with a long lance to make sure he was dead on the cross. Years later at Masada, Longinus was in charge of the Roman legion that had come to imprison the Jewish rebels that refused to give allegiance to Rome. Under the "Pax Romana" if you didn't openly defy Rome, or cause too much civil disturbance, or try to incite others to treason, Rome let you live. That was considered quite fair and understanding in those days. Since the Jews on the cliffs of Masada refused to bend the knee or bow to Rome, their nuisance factor was deemed sufficient to lay siege until they surrendered. Longinus decided to starve them out. After more than the better part of a year, the women and children that had survived were so emaciated that their leader decided to Monty Hall it, and cried out, "let's make a deal." Longinus promised him safe passage down to him under a white flag of truce. When they finished arguing terms, they couldn't come to any agreement. Longinus offered unconditional surrender and life, or death as an alternative. Drawing a circle around Judas Macabee with his spear in the sand he said, "Take as long as you like to decide your course of action, but don't leave the safety of the circle or I will kill you. When Judas complained about the betrayal since he was offered safe passage under the truce of a white flag, Longinus replied, "I only offered you safe passage down here to me, not your return."

I pointed out to Larry his deal was infinitely better than the people at Masada had received. He thereafter capitulated. We went on bended knee and both survived. It was not the kind of deal I ever want to be involved with in the future. Sometimes you just have to confess the error of your ways and start over because when the music stops playing, you have to put your arms down.

Ray shared a story with us that I will share with all of you. It was enlightening to both Larry and Me. Ray decided to enlarge the profits of the tribe, so he and his family took a trip to Spokane, Washington to examine the possibility of expanding their sphere of influence and building greater cash flow for everybody. Things looked so promising that they bought land and built a huge casino. They then ordered slot machines, roulette tables, a Faro Wheel, Chuck-A-Luck, black jack tables and the whole shooting match to bring professional gambling to Spokane, Las Vegas style. They spent hundreds of thousands of dollars to make the dream become a reality. It took several trips and lots of planning. Everything looked like it was a done deal, a real shoe-in. They only forgot one thing. They didn't ask permission from any of the players that had arrived there before them.

Ray rented a van. He and his two big bodyguard sons went to Spokane to take delivery of the equipment. His beautiful daughter went with him. She became impatient that everything took so long. She was really, really bored waiting for the equipment to arrive and be set up, so her dad rented her a car and she decided to run into town on a beer run for the boys. When she didn't come back for twenty-four hours, they knew something was wrong.

A voice on Rays private cell phone that he never gave out to anyone but family members said, "Ray this is a friend of yours, I'm calling to let you know that we think your daughter is going to be okay, but we need to show you something before we can decide that. Tell your sons to keep their guns in their holsters and we will come and talk to you if that is what you want us to do."

Ray said it was what he wanted. He said a few minutes later a beautiful Rolls Royce showed up at their motel that they were staying at. He said four men got out of the car elegantly dressed. They knocked on his door and Ray invited them in.

Their spokesperson said, "Ray, everybody makes mistakes. We all hope we don't make too many we can't recover from. Your daughter made a mistake and we were able to save her this time." He pulled out an 8"X10" photograph of Cindy's rental car T-boned in the middle by a garbage truck. Ray was speechless. "We cancelled your equipment order. You probably made a mistake and thought no one was here tending the store, but Ray, we forgive you and there are no hard feelings. We just chalked it up to experience and hope you do the same thing. We aren't ready for Vegas style gambling here yet. You go home where you belong and we will forget this whole thing ever happened."

Ray told Larry with great solemnity, "Sometimes, you just have to admit the other guy has beat you and take your marbles and go home, if you want to keep on living that is. I've heard some guys have a death wish and just don't know when to quit. You're not one of those guys are you, Larry?"

Larry shook his head no and we left with our hats in our hands and our hearts in our throats. Larry got to keep the fireworks, and the money from the salmon he stole, but he hasn't been able to get a job with the tribe ever since. And it's probably better that he doesn't tempt himself beyond his ability to resist any more than he has to. Incidentally, the Puyallup tribe has 2,713 registered members who will each get a payout of $98,000 per year from the tribe's investments. I think for the first time maybe the Indians finally beat the White man at his own game, but if you don't agree with that, they have an open invitation for you to come and try your luck any time you feel lucky enough to beat them at their own game in their own casino. I can almost hear them yelling now, "Come on down with your hair flying back."

A JEWISH ANGEL

One day when my wife had her charity, I received a call from a little Jewish guy named Leo Wiseman. I didn't know him and he didn't want to talk on the phone, he had a phobia about big brother listening in on us. I agreed to meet him in a suburb of Seattle called SeaTac. I didn't go there much because it only had the airport and peripheral businesses that all metropolitan airports seem to have.

When I arrived, there was this nervous little guy pacing up and down. He was waiting outside a huge Quonset hut a block long. He was wearing clothes from the fifties and pants and a shirt that were polyester. Now, I am no fashion maven, but if I noticed it, I figured everyone else did, too. I was early for our appointment so I was surprised to see him edgy about the time factor. He approached to within three feet of me and told me his name. I gave him mine. He religiously kept the three feet between us because he could smell my wife's cigarette smoke on me. He wanted to know if we helped kids. I replied, "Yes."

He then told me a crushing story. He was born a poor Jew in Ballard, Washington. His dad was a merchant. He went to school with Swedes, Norwegians, Poles and every other denomination that likes to make fun of Jews. He was small and frail. Guess who they all liked to beat up and make fun of? His first bike he found broken under the Fremont Bridge. He hand pounded the wheel back into a semi-round shape. It was egg shaped, but it could be ridden which was better than walking. He rode it to school ever day all through high school. He was a constant object of ridicule. He wore old hand me down clothes. The depression almost killed his family off. He lost his mother and father. They were sick and couldn't afford medicine. They died of what was popularly called consumption in those days. In reality, it was probably malnutrition and heart break.

Leo survived and was drafted to go to war. He was smart and saw the army as an upgrade in living. After basic training they sent him to the Capitol Building of the United States in Washington D.C. He was in charge of raising and lowering the flag every day. He loved his job and was immensely proud to be an American. When he got out of the U.S. Army, he returned to Seattle to find his brother and sister. He had saved his army paychecks diligently. He had a little nest egg he had carefully saved up. He used it to buy a small piece of property with two ramshackle houses on it. He moved his remaining family into them.

He started buying things no one else wanted. He fixed and cleaned and sold them until he acquired quite a lot of items. He had a five-minute timer attached to his lapel. He would set it for five minutes at a time whenever you talked to him, because time was precious and he didn't want to waste any of it. He was very time conscious.

To skip ahead in the next three years, Leo gave me an education in life that I couldn't have gotten in any accredited university on earth anywhere. He unlocked one of two quonset huts and as I walked through, he told me to make a list of anything the children could use or needed: toys, or gifts for Christmas. I was astonished at the plethora of things he had inside his cave of treasures. He had no inventory, he said, because he didn't want to count things, or evaluate them, because his heart might get changed and his desire to have things might sway him in his desire to help anyone he chose for the rest of his remaining life. He especially wanted to help kids.

I will only name a few of the things Leo shared with me in the next three years. Leo knew most of Seattle's homeless people by name. He wandered among them at night when they crouched in doorways or lay down in abandoned buildings. He bought every sleeping bag he could get from dry cleaners, salvage places, Good Will, and even new if he had to. He distributed them as needed. He never wanted recognition, or thanks. He made the city put up chemical toilets downtown for the downtrodden when the city just wanted to arrest them. He bought fifteen hundred pairs of shoes and distributed them to the homeless. He paid for food in every Burger King that refused to serve the homeless and drove them out of doors in bad weather because they smelled, were unkempt and drove away paying customers. Leo made arrangements with the Bon Marche to fix the shoes of any homeless person that needed it.

I haven't seen Leo for awhile, but I know that this little nervous man is a giant in my book. Lots of people on the streets don't even know his name. He is just the sickly guy with the battered old van that drives up in the dead of night that gives you something out of his van if you need it. I never met, or knew Mother Teresa, but I know she and Leo would have understood and liked each other.

I'm sure the city of Seattle wishes he would move on to another city. I'll bet the mayors office wishes he would just die and leave them alone. But I'm here to tell you that when I asked him why did he bother himself with it all these years, I even told him that most people didn't appreciate what he did for them. They didn't even know his name or care who he was.

He said, "I'm not doing it for them. I'm doing it for me. The world is unbalanced. There are too many poor people. I can't help them all, but I was lucky to be born in the richest nation on earth, I'm going to help as many as I can before I die and maybe some more after I'm dead. I owe this country a great debt I can never repay in its entirety, but I can sure make a hell of a dent in it." Then he laughed. And it felt good to stand next to him and laugh with him.

I am proud to say that in my travels I have occasionally met men of substance and influence, but I never met another man that could even touch shoulders with Leo Weisman, a lonely forgotten Jew I met and knew on the mean streets of Seattle. He was and is a giant among men, an angel in disguise, if there ever was one.

MILTON BALLARD

Milton Ballard called me on the phone. Since I was in the money business, I was used to people calling me that I didn't know, or have a clue as to who they were. However, when I returned Milton's call he acted like I should know who he was and what he wanted. Now I have a pretty good memory, but I didn't recall ever talking to this guy before, nor did I recognize his voice. So naturally I asked him what he wanted me for.

He said, "Well, I'm not stupid enough to tell you on the phone," and he got a little huffy with me.

I got irritated and told him, "Well, if it's a secret, keep it to yourself. I don't have time to play guessing games with you on the phone," and I hung up. After all, he dialed me I didn't call him.

The next day he called back and he was a little friendlier so I was, too. He asked me if I knew where Ballard Marina was. I guessed in Ballard. "Exactly," he replied. It had his name on it because he owned it. Now I didn't know a lot about marinas except that they involved boats, water and money.

So I went to see him. I rang the bell on his office and pretty soon a big lumberjack guy dressed in a flannel shirt with big boots came to the door and answered it. I identified myself and he invited me inside his office. It was paneled in wood and looked warm, cozy and rich. He pushed a button and asked for someone to send Frank in. He made small talk and offered me coffee, tea or soup. Pretty soon a very large man came in, locked the door behind him, and stood in front of it at attention like some huge marine. Now, I get a little nervous with locked doors, guards and other such formalities ever since my prison experience.

"What's with the muscle?" I asked?

He played it off with, "Oh! Frank just protects my interests, is all."

"What's the deal?" I asked.

He responded by opening a drawer in his desk and pulling out twenty five thousand dollars still in the bank wrappers. He pushed it across the desk to me and said, "This is yours plus another twenty five thousand just like it when you finish the job."

I expressed surprise. "What job are you talking about you? You haven't told me what you want me to do for you yet." He seemed chastened and angry at the same time. He pulled out an eight by seven photo of a reasonably attractive middle-aged woman. "What's this about?" I asked.

"You get the other twenty five thousand dollars when this woman has a fatal accident," he explained.

"You've got the wrong guy" I exclaimed. "I don't do that kind of work."

"Well, you know people who do," he said.

"Well, I sure as hell am not going to introduce you to them, so tell your boy to move I'm leaving here." I pushed the money and the picture back across the desk to him. As I got up to leave I fliply told him, "Buy yourself a Soldier of Fortune magazine. They have guys that go anywhere to whack anyone anytime anywhere any place."

I left and figured I'd never see or hear from the guy again. When much to my surprise I picked up my morning newspaper a few months later and there as Paul Harvey would say "Was the rest of the story!" It seems Milton did buy a Soldier of Fortune Magazine and wrote to one of the advertisers. A guy showed up with tattoos and scars. He took the contract. He showed up later with a ten by twelve glossy photo of Milton Ballard's wife laying dead in her own blood and gore. When Milton went to pay the other twenty five thousand dollars, the guy yelled, "I'm with the F.B.I. you're under arrest for solicitation to commit murder"! The rest is history. Milton is doing fifteen years to life in Walla Walla penitentiary. He learned that thinking it, leads to doing it.

Then like Robert Blake learned too late, no matter how much money you have, the court and its officers in collusion with attorneys will punish you until it's all gone. Even O.J. Simpson learned the agony goes and on until the money is gone. They all will assure you it's nothing personal, it's just them doing their job. Their job is to make your life more interesting until the money is gone. Then you still get to do the time. Don't do the crime if you can't do the time is the law, not just a good or highly relevant idea.

THE RIGHT REVEREND RON SMITH

The phone rang and when I picked it up the caller introduced himself as the Right Reverend Ron Smith. Now I don't mind people using their appellation as though it is their first name. President Bush and the Queen of England often introduce themselves by their titles, but since I was nobody important, why would anyone try to overwhelm me with a title. I secretly know I'm barely important enough to respond to a simple "hey, dude, or yo buddy." Such formalities put me on my guard automatically.

Americans have the worst telephone manners in the world anyway. The British have the best telephone etiquette. They call you, and they identify themselves, and ask for the party they wish to talk to, and tell whoever answers the phone what the call is about. In case you want to alert the person being called, or to give them a heads up, as it were, Americans allow absolutely no time to interrupt your personal internal dialogue, or your personal stream of consciousness. They just start talking and leave it up to the person receiving the call to sort out who it is, and what the subject or the call is about.

Maybe it's because Alexander Graham Bell got us all off to a bad start with that first telephone call. By answering "Ahoy," instead of saying "hello"…That is probably why so many telephone sales calls fail. They Say Sampson of the Bible killed more than two thousand Philistines with the jawbone of an ass, and that most sales are killed with the same weapon.

The Right Reverend Ron Smith wanted to borrow seven hundred fifty thousand dollars and wanted to know would I get it for him? And how much would I charge him for my services? Naturally I asked him the telling questions every lender wants to know. i.e. "How much money is needed? How long is the term of the loan?" What is the purpose of the loan? What is the method of Payback (the most important item) and finally what collateral is offered to secure the loan?" A lender can usually withstand to lose some interest. It is the lenders profit. But no lender can afford to lose his principal. The Reverend Ron seemed talkative but responsive on the phone so I agreed to meet him later that day at a restaurant in the suburbs of Seattle that he hand picked. I tried telling him church people were bad financial risks. Conventional lenders don't like them because they don't have reliable track records of borrowing and paying back loans. They don't want to foreclose on a church because it's bad press, and makes the lender look like a heartless Simon Legree taking their pound of flesh to get paid. In addition to that, most churches usually have very limited cash flow. It is unpredictable in its amount of return," The church can't foretell how much usable income it will have to pay back the lender with since much of it is received by voluntary donations. Now there are some notable exceptions to these rules. I have successfully gotten some rare churches qualified to borrow substantial amounts of money from ethical lenders, but I never tell that to a would be, "I'm a man of God, can you spare me a few million bucks for God?"

Part of it is because of the typical attitude they display upon meeting you. The first hurdle is: the I know God personally syndrome, and I have an autographed picture of God in my wallet. If we do a deal together I may show it to you. It's been my experience that as soon as these guys have to do any show and tell, they forgot their wallet. They come as close to living free as anybody can muster. Secondly, it's their I'm special. I deserve special consideration apart from the rest of humanity. I never lied and you have my word on that.

The real good guys like Benny Hinn, Billy Graham, or Oral Roberts, would never be caught dead talking to riff raff like me. They have personal financial people that can make numbers sing like the Mormon Tabernacle Choir. Jim Baker, after he was exposed, turned out to be a hell of a number's cruncher. He may not have known the Bible as far as application in his personal life, but buddy, when he got through with your wallet you realized the secret money compartment was now empty and you just bought a first class one-way ticket to heaven. It's too bad he had to ride coach class to that other place he went to. It worked out pretty good for Jessica Hahn, Tammy Faye, Ross and some of the other church helper bees though. They say it's an ill wind that doesn't blow someone some good. I heard that is how Oklahoma acquired a lot of that Texas farmland. A big wind blew it to them. Besides, Jim Baker learned to respect, like and rely on large black inmates named Bubba and Leroy.

Well, I had my first meeting with the right reverend Ron Smith and it was a skosh different than I thought it would be. He had just spent forty-two years growing up high in the hidden villages of a remote canton in the Peoples Republic of China. His parents had moved there from Seattle. They sold all their worldly possessions and turned their lives over to God. They labored among obscure people in an obscure province. Now Ron had returned to Seattle to borrow money to help many, many, many, let me say that one more time many people. He was fluent in the Hoiken dialect. I was impressed with that, but when I asked the telling question, if you go back to China, how does the lender get paid? He seemed puzzled by this. Well, I will give you my personal word on it he said. I told him, I don't make the loan. I don't have any money. The lender will want a little more than just your word and a handshake. He then wanted to submit letters from Chinese people that all said he was a good guy. I explained I couldn't do the deal. I didn't know anyone who could. etc. etc. It's like the guy was stone deaf. He offered me twenty five thousand dollars on the back end and hinted he would go to up to fifty thousand dollars. I explained again that I'd just be paying myself. What do I need you for?

I hoped that would quench his fire, crush his desire, and maybe disillusion him entirely.

Instead, he pulled out five thousand dollars in cash and handed it to me. "Do the best you can" he said. I handed it back and asked where he got it? He said, "Bank of America loaned him enough to buy a new T-Bird, start a church here in Seattle and find a place to live. When I asked what did you give as collateral the answer nearly knocked me out of my chair. "Nothing," he said. "They were sympathetic to my plight."

It wasn't until I raced through his answer in my mind that I dared to ask the next question. "Ron, which branch did you go through?" When he told me the main branch in China Town, I knew how he did it, but I was not sure he was playing with a full deck. I asked if they conducted the business in English, or Chinese. He said, "In English, but what difference did it make?"

I explained that he had just made a loan from the Chinese Tong. He went pale on me and began to tremble a little. He had lived in China long enough to know that of the two thousand Triad Heaven and Earth societies that exist, the benevolent order of Tong carry out the orders of the society. He had unknowingly forfeited not only his own life, but also the life of every living relative anywhere on earth down to the fourth generation. His body and theirs were collateral for the loan. These orders and secret societies have existed for centuries. They make the Italian Mafia look like preschool, or day care by comparison. I told him he needed my help more than he knew. I advised him to return the money immediately. He refused. I explained perhaps I could go to a man I knew who ran the Hong Kong Shangai bank in Seattle. That if I implored Rodney the manager just right, he may extend him a revolving line of credit large enough to act as bridge capital; he could then pay off the Tong and have a fresh source of revenue that didn't have such high stakes attached to it. He finally agreed to this. I had him meet me the next day, did the necessary introductions, and took a fee of fifty dollars for my time and trouble.

He had his T-Bird. He found a place to practice church, and a place to live. I think attorneys practice, Doctors practice, and so do church people. I figured that would keep him busy and I would never see the guy again. Boy, was I ever wrong. I cruised by his church once in awhile over on 125th Street and usually saw his T-Bird parked right in front of the church. Then after eight months passed, I didn't see the car there anymore and I figured he must have gone back to China. It wasn't until the leaves had fallen from the trees and Halloween approached that I spotted the car hidden in a neatly carved alcove in the blackberry bushes with a screen of cut tree branches over it. I smelled a rat.

Two weeks later I called a successful finance and loan guy I know who lives a very circumspect life. I invited him to lunch in Chinatown. I just didn't tell him the owner of the seven seas had a lingerie show there once a year. I knew Kevin's wife wouldn't approve of him seeing nubile young models offering the latest in lingerie while dining on some of the best food in Chinatown. It was worth it to see his reaction when the first model walked out of the back room and in between the tables where we were eating. He almost stabbed his eyes out with the chopsticks he was struggling with. When I went to pay the bill, the owner of the restaurant bowed very low and asked to talk to me in private for a moment. I excused myself and went into a back room. He asked me as a favor to appear at a loan signing the next night. It would be held in the Temple above the Bank of America. I inquired around and found out it was an old client of mine doing the loan, but I was puzzled because no matter how good my standing among the orientals, it didn't require an occidental's approval to do a Chinese loan. I went the next night and, lo and behold, it was the Right Reverend Ron Smith borrowing four hundred fifty thousand dollars from the Tong family. I couldn't believe my eyes. The papers were already drawn. The officers had already signed; the money lay on the table in the bank wrappers. Ron wasn't at all ill at ease or nervous about the deal. I didn't dare take a fee. I told him not to do the deal. He swore he wouldn't. Then he went over to the table and signed the papers. I was totally mystified and excused myself.

A short time thereafter I was stopped on a downtown Seattle street by a man I didn't know. He handed me a crisp one hundred dollar bill. I reluctantly took the money and asked him what it was for? I was told that it was for being the voice of warning to the borrower, that I had played my part perfectly.

That relieved me somewhat. But I know this, if Ron is still alive somewhere in the world. He must be looking over his shoulder behind him. I know I would be. In China they say, "There is a short distance between the smile and the knife." Sometimes orientals can be very inscrutable, but I learned, so can preacher men. If you know what I mean.

THE DATING GAME

Every time I start to think I've heard and seen it all and there are no new surprises anyone can show me, Satan pulls the rug out from under me.

At least I like to attribute it to Satan. That excuse worked well for Flip Wilson. As Georgina his lady in drag used to say, "The devil made him do it." And Dana Carvey made it work for him with his church lady shtick that he did so well.

I had a friend that liked to go to singles events in the hope of meeting miss perfect. My argument with that scenario is if you met someone that was perfect they wouldn't want you. It seemed to fall on deaf ears. I attended quite a few singles events with him since I'm prone to sitting back and watching others before I commit to anything. Nobody overwhelmed me, or I them. My friend danced with and chatted up anyone who would let him. We were polar extremes.

I found out after going to what seemed like thirty eleven of these events that I wasn't doing it right. You're supposed to get on the internet and assume a cool moniker, or handle like (Flaming Drawers) Lovey craves it, or cokebottle if you were a girl. Guys had names like Big Huggy Bear, Cuddles, fuzzy face, or puppy luv. I thought I was going to be sick. I watched him do this week after week and I could tell I was destined to stay single for a long time to come, so as a prank I wrote my own add. It read thusly…"Hard as nails, hopelessly cruel man looking for vulnerable women to exploit". Sixty-nine women answered my advertisement. I couldn't believe the response to my ad.

I called some of the women at random and they said they enjoyed my candor and forthrightness. That scared me even more. I went out with a few of them just for a change of pace. It was a change of life that I wasn't ready for. The first girl I met greeted me with, "Hi, I'm Laura, just so there is no confusion I don't care where we go, or what we do, but I never have sex on the first date."

Naturally my automatic rejoinder was, "Then let's just skip this date and pretend were going out for the second time." That one definitely threw her. She kept puzzling over it all evening. I like a girl that has a clear view of what her priorities are.

I moved on down the list. The next girl I met I liked to call whips and chains. Her shtick was a version of tie me up, whip me, beat me, and make me write bad checks. She was a one-date adventure, also.

However, date number three was the one that rang my chimes. She was a vampire. She explained that she didn't drink blood, but she drained men of their vitality, and hospitalized them with sex. Besides dancing with the devil, she needed someone to teach her how to walk on fire, stop their heart at will, jump out of airplanes etc. She had hooked up with a group that did all that stuff and more. I just had to investigate her further. So I went with her to the fire walk. It was real cool. Then we did the four-minute under water thing. We did the mastering our body rhythm thing, and the sensory deprivation thing in the floating salt-water tank. We did the self-hypnosis thing. We did the camping with just a knife and matches thing. We attended the guardian angels classes and learned how to leap out of a speeding van onto a bad guy and throw them to the ground and handcuff them. It was all grist for her mill, but I skipped the lets have sex until you're hospitalized thing.

The girl had a guy panting over her that I wanted to meet. He raised unicorns and sold them. His name was Otter Zell. He was a cryptozooligist. He studied extinct animals and tried to find new ones. Well, Otter Zell was unusual to say the least. I was getting ready to write him off entirely, when Lysette invited me to spend a weekend with her and Otter at his compound in California. Naturally, I went.

It turned out the guy was more of a scientist than I realized. He was cloning animals years before geneticists manufactured Dolly the sheep. Otter had some baby goats. When the babies were born, he transplanted the horn cap at just the right moment so that the two horns grew together and spiraled upward out of the animal's forehead. They looked just like little shaggy ponies with a unicorn head. Otter shot himself in the foot or hoof though. He sold an exclusive four unicorns to Barnum and Bailey Circus with a non-competition agreement. He couldn't sell anymore to anyone else.

He next planned to capture a mermaid. It seems Fiji had a bunch of the elusive little critters. I knew this guy who had more money than brains, so I introduced the two of them to each other. Mr. Cash & Carry put up two hundred fifty thousand dollars for Otter to fly to Fiji with a camera crew to film a documentary movie on the Mermaids of the Fiji Islands. Well, Otter was gone for a few months and I kind of laid the matter to rest. I only thought of it when Lysette, my vampire lady, would call to tell me about her latest conquest that she had hospitalized with sex. She would then ask me about Otter and his project.

I got a call after several months and it seems Otter Zell was back. He wanted to tell me the saga of the Fiji mermaids and how he had gotten himself deported persona non-grata. Otter, it seems, was having trouble getting the little buggers to show up under good filming conditions. They only showed up at dusk on the outer reef of the atoll. I guess he became tired of waiting or his visa expired. He shot and killed one of them. He had it on ice when one of the locals saw it propped up in a tent with a stick under its chin. The locals consider them sacred. They call them "RI" which is pronounced Rhee. In the movie that he showed me, they looked like aquatic primates. They have a fold of skin under each arm that extends when they extend their arms, which are quite long for a creature of that size. They have webbed fingers and toes. Their mouth is round with very thin external lips. They have long hair with algae growing in it, which makes it look green. Their nostrils are just two occluded holes with no visible protuberance like we have. It seems Otter was bringing the body back to the United States when customs waylaid him and locked him down. They took the body of the RI, as it is a national treasure to them, but they let him keep his movie footage.

I thought I knew pretty much every creature living on this planet. I watch Discovery channel faithfully, but like I told you earlier, every time I think I have all the answers life has to offer me, someone pulls the rug out from underneath my understanding.

Otter is now searching for a dinosaur in Africa. I'm waiting for that one with bated breath. He wants to capture one alive. My grandfather used to tell me if someone eats a lemon in front of you and wants to bet you he can squirt lemonade from his eyes by pursing his lips, you better not bet him and you better back up or you're going to get wet. Who knows, with a name and profession like his, he Otter find one.

TINY EDWARDS

Tiny Edwards was a taxicab driver. He owned his own cab in collusion with three other guys. They ran the wheels off that rig. It was in service twenty-four hours a day. It was a yellow cab and so were they. Tiny weighed five hundred pounds plus. The other three behemoths that claimed ownership could pass for almost normal. That is, if you ignored their jailhouse tattoos, the stench of unwashed bodies, and clothes that reeked from not being washed in so long...that they could stand in the corner by themselves whenever they were pried off their squalid bodies. The Romans used the word vulgar for the unclean, unwashed, uneducated masses. That would have fit these guys to a T.

When you call for a taxicab, you get what you get. It's usually too late when you climb in the cab and find Satan at the wheel. They had a backup cab waiting to be fixed, so if their primary cab went down for mechanical repairs, they were not out of business. They would usually park both cars on their front lawn in Ballard and wait until they sold some drugs to have enough money to buy parts. Then the fighting would begin. Major issues had to be resolved, things like diagnosis of what caused the car not to go, what parts were needed, how to get to the parts house, who had to go to the parts house, and who was going to fix it, or better yet, who could or knew how to fix it. Usually they would get someone who was a part of their drug culture to solve all the problems aforementioned by giving them drugs to do it for them.

The thing that amazed me was that these guys had mothers, who wanted to lay claim to birthing them, let alone knowing them. These were not jolly men, but yellow cab had the master license and as long as you have paid the State of Washington two hundred thousand dollars for a ticket to drive on the states highways, you keep as many cabs running as you can. It costs you the same either way, plus, every cabbie has to bust the NUT every day to make money. The NUT is the fee the cab company charges the driver to drive his cab. It's about sixty-five dollars per day in Seattle. It's a lot more than that in Chicago and New York City.

Now Ballard, Washington is where everybody either buys drugs, raises drugs or sells drugs. It's where everybody goes to party on the weekend. It used to be a fishing town inhabited by really tough men who were either Norwegian, or Swedish by extraction. Since those early days Bardhal oil has come into town, so have fast food joints and high schools. (Some people spell it HI-schools), a junkyard, a lumberyard and some fringe businesses. (You know witchcraft, sand candle, incense, and crystal new age shops.) The old days where you had a bowl of clam chowder and drank "Boy Howdy Ya yeah Betcha Beer," or had ludafisque and Lingon berries are gone. The boat builders are still there and the Ballard locks still let the boats out to sea and back in again. There is a harbor and a yacht basin for the very wealthy, but they are the exception and not the rule. The place has been re-sold many times. Yuppies and stoners have taken over most of the affordable housing. If you're lucky, you converted your old sea shanty with partitions and rent it out to college students, usually four to six students at a time. You charge big front end deposits because you know they are going to come and go without a minutes notice. Plus, there will be damage and repainting repairs. That is a given from the get go. A house you bought for twenty eight thousand dollars in nineteen forty five can be rented out for three thousand two hundred dollars per month, not a bad deal if you think about it. Meanwhile, you struggle to meet code on a fixer upper house you are living in and when it's finished you're in fat city.

The reason I tell you all this before I relate the details of how I came by this knowledge is I had heard for years about some cab drivers that owned slaves living in Ballard somewhere, but I had not crossed their paths in all my inter city travels and just took it to be a typical urban legend. A story that as Abraham Lincoln used to say "Lost nothing in the telling."

One hot August morning I had a furtive phone call. A young girls voice whispered, "You have to help me, please help me, I'm trapped at Tiny Edwards house. He has men guarding me night and day so I can't escape. He killed a man last night and he swears he will kill me too, if I try to escape. Come quickly or it will be too late.

I believed her. There is something about the truth that dispels all doubt and cuts through the smog and the haze that most communication struggles with. "Who is this?" I asked.

"I'm Susan," came the fervent reply. "I met you up on Broadway with Tina boosting stuff from Fred Meyer about a year ago."

I suddenly remembered her. I had made them put everything back, or I threatened to turn them into security. Funny how circumstances can bring you new friends when the need is great enough. I guess the need was great enough. I obtained an address from her and went to meet the man of her dreams. Too bad they were all nightmares and the guy turned out to be Freddie Kruger.

When I arrived there, I cruised the street first to make sure I wasn't being set up. Both yellow cabs were up on the lawn with the hoods up. This is usually a sign of distress. I walked up to the house so I couldn't be seen through the big front window, by approaching it from the neighbor's side. Now when you ring a doorbell you expect someone to come to the door and ask if they can help you, or inquire as to what you want. I could have been anybody, but I wasn't. I was dressed in Levi jeans and a t-shirt. It was already eighty degrees and rising. I may have told you before but at the risk of repeating myself (something I rarely do) smile. I don't like the heat! Even though it was quiet and I heard no interior noise, I listened before I rang the bell for several minutes.

Most people surround themselves with noise. They can't seem to enjoy anything that is too quiet. My wife surrounds herself with country noise. The twang plays in her brain twenty-four hours a day, sometimes simultaneously while the T.V. is playing. There was no interior noise. My mind started racing. I'm a target; I've missed them or I have the wrong address. The girl was pretty shook up and scared. She could have transposed a number or misinformed me. Then you sort it out and say to yourself, naw, too many coincidences "This is the place," as Brigham Young would have said if he had been there.

Just then the door was violently jerked opened by a five hundred pound gorilla with a gun in his hand. All I saw was Shamu the whale with a gun. Your instincts take over and your survival skills come into play or you perish. I snatched the gun out of his hand and pounded him on the forehead with the butt end of the pistol with every ounce of strength my hundred and eighty-pound body could muster. He fell backward partly inside his own doorstep. He was out cold. The dull cracking sound like a bowling ball being dropped on a watermelon had me worried though. What if I'd inadvertently killed the guy? As a convicted felon I wouldn't be able to get any jury in the land to believe my story. Just then Mr. Edwards let out a huge moan and tried to heave himself to a sitting position. Meanwhile, the sweet smell of budding marijuana was pouring out of the house in a wave. I almost got a contact high just being there. No wonder the dude was so defensive.

Before he could open his eyes and focus them properly I asked him "Where is the girl?"

"Which one?" He asked.

"How many do you have?" I queried. "Three or four," he answered nonchalantly. "Which one do you want?"

"Sue" I replied.

"Well, hell," he said, "I was getting tired of her anyway you can have her, but she still owes me sixty five dollars that she has to work off."

362

I saw red. I fired the little gun slightly above his head and to the right. It hit his fish bowl and bounced into the bookcase. It was only a twenty-two. Then I remembered and realized twenty-two bullets can kill people, too. It just looked small in his big meaty paw. I took all the girls and his little gun.

He swore he would find me and kill me. I used to get two or three of those threats in prison every day. It was a slow day if you didn't have a couple of death threats by noon. I told him, "I know about the Navy guy you iced under the monorail last night. Don't make me drop a dime on you. I'll call Mr. BoBo and *the man* will finish you." It's funny how the truth just cuts through everything. I got one of those crazy insights that just comes out of nowhere. "Better yet, I predict that within three days you will be burned all over that fat, ugly, mean spirited body of yours and I will come and visit you in the hospital. Your days of hurting people are over."

It was over one hundred two degrees three days later. When Tiny's cab overheated up on Capitol Hill, not six blocks from Harborview Hospital, he got out of the cab, raised the hood and heard sizzling sounds. Since some stoner had repaired the cab, they mutually decided they didn't need to hook the temperature-sending gage back up. Tiny had no warning whatsoever when he took off his T-shirt to take off the radiator cap that had burned his hand when he first tried it. With the shirt to insulate his hand from the heat, he turned the cap just enough to bring old faithful into service. The geyser of steaming four hundred eighty degree water and anti-freeze burned him over all his upper body. He was lucky to be so close to Harborview Hospital. They have one of the best burn wards in the United States. They saved his life. I went to visit him four days later. The hospital said I wasn't on his visitors list. I told them I was family, but he started screaming and became so upset they made me leave. I went back later that night. Night shifts are notoriously lax. I took him a peace offering, a cup of hot chili from Wendys. I threw a little extra spice in it just in case it wasn't hot enough for him. When I woke him up, he didn't seem glad to see me. He started yelling again so I had to excuse myself and leave. I never went back to see if Tiny ate his chili, but I think some people would complain if you hung them with a brand new rope.

I know this though, Tiny Edwards doesn't drive cab anymore, and his slave driving ways are over. He moved back to Minnesota where many are cold, but few are frozen. So my motto from all this is, to parents like Tiny, do what the Greeks did with unwanted children. Just put them quietly to sleep in the snow and never go back for them. If you raise a monster be careful because they might outlive you and they get to choose your new home when you are old and feeble.

AB AND THE LAZY "B"

Ab Mobasher was born in Iran. His family was wealthy even by Middle Eastern standards. He was born with a silver spoon in his mouth and a nurse to feed him with it. The family had amassed their fortune by being rug merchants. Some of the finest rugs in the world are woven in Iran. Even under the Shah they prospered immeasurably. When we are born into our primary family it is the only world we know. We are born into a pre-established culture. Ab was raised Muslim and observed the strictest rites of propriety. He had two older brothers and two older sisters. He had the finest education money could buy. He associated with other privileged families and played with other privileged children, but his family was at the top of the mountain, so to speak.

When he became old enough, he entered into an obligatory two-year service in the military. He was posted to a remote mountain top outpost far removed from the family he dearly loved. Ab faithfully served his term in the military and returned home to find that his beloved father, the family patriarch, had died. Nobody had notified him they said because they didn't want to disturb his military duty. They managed to settle the estate without him and because he was the youngest he received nothing. His mother and older brothers inherited the bulk of the estate. He was told he could come to the homestead for dinner once a week, but there was no money for further education, investment, or work opportunity. In fact, they strongly urged him to leave the country because of the abdication of the peacock throne by the Shah of Iran.

Ab took their advice and moved to Texas. He found work as a graphic artist and tool and die man. He had great skill and ability at consulting and advising business people that wanted to try new adventures, but he had one major fault that he still has to this day. He trusted people. He kept working for free on borrowed promises that if he made other people rich, they would reward him later for his service to them. There is an old joke on the curb of life. How do they say, "screw you" in California? The answer is "TRUST ME!"

After awhile he learned how to ask for some money up front. That helped him get the job of making model space ships for Gene Rodenberry and the show Star Trek. They really are pretty cool models. They are bigger than you think and they photograph well when they are slid along a wire that runs clear across the studio.

When I met Ab he was working for Boeing aircraft as a tool and die man. When the lazy B found out Ab would work an infinite number of hours, they worked that boy around the clock. He was meeting himself getting up each day. He thought he couldn't say no to their imperatives. He finally had a nervous breakdown. Even Boeings doctors decided that a hundred ten hours a week might be a little too much for the average human to take. They let him cut back to seventy hours a week to let him rest up, so he could recover and go back to his full schedule again.

While Ab was recuperating, he listened to the radio at night, especially Art Bell, a talk show moderator that attracted every weirdo between Mars and Venus. One of the Venusian women got ahold of Ab and convinced him she was an angel from another planet. She had a school of healing with crystal therapy, herb therapy, and massage therapy, warm bath therapy, and the let's get naked and make each other feel good therapy.

Her two teenage sons liked and subscribed to the herb therapy the most. Her boys didn't go to school because the world is wicked and their angel mom didn't want her sons corrupted by Satan's evil minions.

The next thing I knew, Ab seduced himself into moving into her compound and her life. It was an exercise in pain and frustration. Ab, who wanted to help all mankind, quit his job and went to work raising money for the Angel full time.

I asked Ab if she could fly, get invisible, walk through walls, turn water into wine, or walk on water. She told him she could but didn't want to expose her full powers because it would make everyone else jealous and then they would interfere with her work. I talked to her on the phone and she told me her work was to acquire as much money as possible without paying taxes on the money. I told her I knew some non-angels that had the same goal in mind, but unfortunately I had met them in federal prison. She didn't think that was funny at all. She tried to recruit me, but I had to work to make a living and I didn't have time to go to the angel ranch and learn the intricacies of candlepower.

Ab had a big dream. I believe he still does. He has designed a huge building. It is what they call a super building. There are some places in the world where they have such buildings where the inhabitants live, work, shop, and recreate themselves all in one complex, or multi-plex. It is an ingenious design, but it would cost a fortune to construct it. The chief problem is you need a culture that has a central axis around which the whole culture revolves.

I told Ab, "That dog won't hunt in America, but maybe he could go back to Iran and it would fly." I understand they have built some super cities in Iran and other parts of the Middle East. Maybe some day, Ab's dream will become a reality, but I don't think it will happen in this lifetime.

Meanwhile, Ab contents himself with subscribing to every new age idea that comes along. He takes every self-help seminar offered. He tried getting married a couple of times, but he later found out that American women are after financial success first. Everything else comes in a distant second. Somewhere he hopes to find an ethereal woman who can live on love without regard for material gain. I told him it won't happen in the immediate future, that he is going to have to get reincarnated quite a few more times and then he will have to go to a different world to accomplish that dream. Ab accused me of being somewhat cynical. I was shocked and chagrined to be thusly accused and falsely labeled. The upshot of all this is…

I am told it's far harder to have wealth and lose it than it is to have never experienced it at all. I only include the episode of Ab in this book to show that regardless of the pressures upon us, we do not have to turn to a life of crime. The sociologist Edwin Sutherland says we need three things to become a criminal. He postulates in his Differential Theory of Criminal Behavior that we need to associate with others that exhibit criminal behavior that the behavior must be defined as profitable, desirable, or rewarding, and we must ourselves try criminal behavior that results in us getting a reward without punishment. I agree with his hypothesis. Think about it, you may agree also.

Segue:

While I was involved with Ab trying to get a different job, I found a MasterCard in downtown Seattle. I have always been a student of the unusual. It appeared to be a Boeing MasterCard. Now I have long been familiar with MBNA, they issue more Master Cards than anyone else in the world. They tried to recruit me once because of my crypto clearance. I refused them the same as I did the C.I.A and any other spy organizations that gathers information and sells it to the highest bidder. I'm not paranoid, just reluctant to spy on people and sell their secrets. I'd much rather do it in an open book. I noticed this was not an MBNA issued card. It was a direct issue to Boeing bankcard without any preset spending limit. I made some polite inquiries around town and found out who ostensibly owned the card.

When I went to return it, I was in for the shock of my life. It belonged to a beautiful raven-haired girl that obviously was living the good life. Her car was a tricked out 750 IL BMW. Her condominium was on the water, and her clothes were all designer label. She invited me in and offered me a drink. I settled for Snap-E-Tom tomato juice. She drank expensive liquor. She seemed nervous. I'm in her place, but she hadn't asked for her card back or how I found her and knew it was hers. I volunteered a little information to prime the pump. She started talking. She was an independent contractor. Boeing only used her when they could not close a big airplane sale with foreign investors. She could buy anything she wanted and it was paid for by Boeing. It took me an hour to get all that out of her. It was like pulling wisdom teeth to get her to divulge that information.

Suddenly, she changed gears on me. "Do you want to go to dinner? I'm starving," she said. "It's my treat."

I took her temperature by asking, "Don't you mean Boeing's treat?"

She cocked one eyebrow and laughed. "No, I'm not putting this on the card, it would attract too many questions."

She changed clothes so I wouldn't stand out so much and we went as we were to a nice quiet place on the waterfront. While we ate she got quiet and contemplative. She asked me what I did for a living and how I found her. I faked my way through. You never give up your sources or you lose them.

She excused herself and said she had to make a phone call. Since I saw her slide a very expensive micro cell phone into her purse, I figured she wanted privacy. She was gone only a few minutes. I stayed on guard in case she had called some bad guys to come and get me. She still hadn't asked for her MasterCard back, which puzzled me. It was worth a thousand dollars on the street no questions asked. I knew she knew that, too. When she rejoined me she seemed more relaxed and forthcoming. She began by asking me if I had ever stumbled into a spider web unexpectently.

I said, "Yes, but I don't follow, where are you going with this?" She then asked if I knew who John Paisley was. I said, "Sure, he's the president of Boeing; everybody knows that.

She said, "I'm involved with him and I can't get free of him. I need you to help me." Obviously, I wondered how? She said, "I'll give you two thousand dollars to get the MasterCard back to him."

I told her that I wanted three thousand. She said, "Okay," without a moment's hesitation. I was only testing her, so I was a little nonplussed that she upped my play so easily.

I dissembled and asked her, "Why don't you just give it back to him yourself? It would have more finality than coming from me."

She said, "I can't do that."

"Why not?" I asked.

"Because he killed his wife for the insurance proceeds. He's in a lot of financial trouble and owes some very bad people a lot of money. He knows that I know this because he caught me reading his insurance policies and that

I knew that his alibi was phony. I think I may be next, I know too much."

Well, beautiful as she was and as good as the dinner was, it was still a lot to swallow in one sitting. I let her drive us back to her place. I asked her if she was willing to give up the good life for whatever followed.

She smiled and said, "I don't have to give up anything. I have investments. Boeing has been good to me. I have made a lot of money with Boeing."

I knew she spoke the truth. It was all fact and no brag as they say out west. Well, the rest is history. I returned Boeing's MasterCard. After security was dismissed, we had a nice long chat, a real heart to heart or as the French say, tete-ta-tete.

He promised not to hurt my new friend. She sent me the three thousand dollars in the mail, and then Phil Condit became the new president of Boeing. But to do so, he had to acquire Harry Stonecipher, his personal pit, bull just so he could be "The Man."

Mr. Paisley eventually got indicted and convicted of murder one and is still serving his time, but it took seven years for all this to play itself out completely. From it I learned once again, "the mill of the Gods grinds slowly but exceedingly fine." Life is a drama. Sometimes you have to reserve judgment until the last act is finished, even if you think you may have seen this play before.

A VICTIM OF SUCCESS

Glen Davis was the picture of success. He had rippling muscles; a world class tan a noble brow, and the aquiline nose of a Roman senator. In fact, without wanting to, he drew attention to himself. He didn't look like he belonged in prison. The fact that he hung out with the murderers in the joint made it even more of a paradox. He didn't look like a killer is supposed to look like.

Inside the joint people gather themselves together with others that they are comfortable with. All the murderers hang out together and usually dominate the weight pile. They try to make their bodies as large and formidable as possible; this scares other bad guys away that might otherwise be willing to see if they could ice them and thereby earn a bad boy reputation. Most murderers are young, between twenty and thirty five years of age, except for gang bangers who are even younger. They usually range between seventeen and twenty-five years of age.

The murderer justifies his position by rationalizing that he faces his victim man to man. It was him or me mentality. The robber justifies his actions by saying I only rob people that have more than me. They can get more stuff. Lots of times their stuff is insured. I don't kill anybody; I just take stuff. The drug addict is sure to try to impress others with the I have a need syndrome. I only steal to get a fix. I'm not violent if they don't resist me. I just want my drugs. In any case they form groups, cliques, or several individuals that they hang out with, just like people outside of prison walls do with each other.

One day Glen dropped by my bunk. Now your bunk number is your address in the joint. It's like the four digits after the zip code on the outside. Your cell number is the zip code you live at and the bunk number is where you can be found. Now, since I wrote writs for guys, researched law cases in the prison library, and had guys signed up to write lonely heart letters to women on the outside, I was used to guys dropping by.

I put aside what I was working on at moment and asked, "Glen, to what do I owe this honor?" I saw him on the yard and in the chow hall, but I never went out of my way to befriend strangers; I let them come to me.

He started slowly, and then accelerated from there. He said, "I used to work for Ben Franklin Savings Bank in Portland, Oregon. I ran their computer programs. It was a two-year executive training program that I went into right out of college. It's eventually what brought me here. I thought I was going to hear the traditional story all the robbers told. Too much money passing through my fingers I decided to snag a few bills and I was caught.

But Glen surprised me. He asked have you ever done something wrong and you expected it to fail, but instead it took off like a rocket and succeeded so wildly that you became a victim of your own success? I couldn't think of any circumstances like that, so I listened to his tale of woe. "I worked for Ben Franklin in their computer facility in Portland. Every day my job was to reconcile all the accounts and their daily activity. Then I sent the back up tape to Seattle to the main headquarters. One day I was daydreaming and I created a fictitious oil account. I even named it ABC Oil Company. I submitted a bill for four hundred dollars and they paid it immediately no questions were asked. So I secured a mailbox address and started paying myself once or twice a week. I just didn't enter the payment to ABC Oil on the back up master tape I sent to Seattle daily. I never spent a dime of the money. I was too scared to do so. Plus, I only did it as a whim, as an idle exercise. It wasn't carefully thought out or planned, but it was so simple it worked. For two years I did this. Then I realized I had four hundred thousand dollars in my account. I thought it was time to unwind the spool of string. I bought a failing grocery store. I bought grocery vans to do deliveries with. I reworked their balance sheet and their financials. The eight years before I bought this store it lost over ninety thousand dollars a year. That is why I bought it. It was a sure loser. Suddenly, it started making money hand over fist. I bought more vans. I expanded the store to use up more capital. Instead, the store started making over thirty thousand dollars a month after expenses, so I bought a failing dry cleaners in the bad section of town. Immediately it started making a ton of money. I bought a losing bowling alley. It became an immediate money magnet. Finally, my wife and I moved. We bought an expensive house to hide our sudden influx of wealth. I bought a corvette, then a Porsche, then a Ferrari. I still had too much money coming in. I scoured the papers for risky businesses that I could be assured of losing money on. Everything I touched turned to gold. I couldn't lose no matter how hard I tried. We went to Las Vegas. I plunged and took wild bets, played craps and roulette, all the high-risk games;

I just kept on winning more and more money. Our first trip I won seven hundred fifty thousand dollars. On our second trip I won four hundred twenty five thousand dollars. I could not get rid of my excess money. I didn't dare just pull the plug on ABC Oil Company or the roof would fall on me.

I saw an ad in USA Today newspaper of a yacht for sale. My plan was fly to Florida; buy the yacht, pay cash. That would unload the three million plus dollars I had accumulated and let me close out the oil company account that was the start of all my problems. It would allow me to discontinue automatic authorized payments to the account and allow me to zero balance it and make it vanish.

It didn't work out that way. My wife and I flew to Florida. We met the sellers of the yacht and got along with them real well. We convinced them we had sold our business, and our real estate and that was why we had so much cash. They were an older retired couple from New York and they were very suspicious that we had so much cash, but money talks and everything else walks. The trouble was we boarded the yacht and they went to dinner to celebrate their success. My wife Diane asked me if I saw the gold coins, diamonds emeralds, and rubies they showed us when they slid the huge cash box out from under their bed. She asked me, "Glen, how much do you think all that was worth?"

I guessed well over a million bucks. We both said it at the same time, "Lets go back and get it."

They had left their window open. There was just a screen in the way. Diane stood as lookout while I slipped inside. I got the gold and the jewels and we sailed away into the sunset. We had a marvelous time sailing home together. Although we were a little nervous, it was like a second honeymoon. We checked the television, listened to the radio and read the newspapers every day. There was no mention of our robbery.

We never heard another word until thirteen months later. The person we bought the yacht from showed up at my work with an F.B.I. agent. It seems the person we robbed was a retired New York City cop. He had stolen those jewels and gold coins from someone else. He couldn't turn us in because they were already stolen property, but he was riding my coat tails to let me know that he wasn't going to let us get away with it. He wanted half of the stuff or the value thereof returned to him. I explained we had fenced everything for ten cents on the dollar and we couldn't give him as much back as he was asking for.

He told me they found the cash box sitting high and dry. When we threw the box in the canal, it was high tide. We didn't realize when the tide went out, it left the box exposed sitting on the mud. Some curious kids found it and returned it to the rightful owners hoping for a reward. Well, I guess the police sweated those kids until they were infants again.

I asked Glen, "How did you get indicted? What's your charge?"

He bit his lower lip and said, "That's why I'm talking to you. I took a day off for Labor Day. It was the first day I had taken off in 4 years. They brought in a temporary who was totally incompetent. She erased several accounts and when they sent the master tape to Seattle, headquarters went into orbit. They began reconstructing the accounts that had been erased. One of them was my ABC Oil Company account. It appeared in the file of accounts we once had and no longer had. They flew in experts from the East coast. Even the treasury boys got in on the act. They used the ghosts that were left on the master discs to prove what I had done, but they don't know how much money changed hands. So I am here on a general theft indictment. They are sweating me to confess and tell them how much money I took. I am telling them the truth when I tell them it burgeoned so fast that I didn't keep track of every dollar. They now want a general figure to charge me with. I can tell Ben Franklin is going to blame me for every loss they have sustained since the first day they began business."

I suggested to Glen that he should cop a plea. Tell them you want to talk to Monty Hall and let's make a deal. He said he was going to do that but there was one little hitch. They were going to indict his wife for the Florida caper. No wonder the guy was worried. His wife and daughter had gone home to live with her parents to escape the heat.

Well, the rest is history...Glen learned to take a beating and he learned to pray fervently. He began imploring God to punish him, but not his wife and child. Of course some detritus inevitably fell on them, but Glen received a relatively light sentence. The last I heard, he had served his time and got out. Whether he rejoined his wife and daughter, I don't know. You rarely get to see the whole picture to its conclusion. I learned from listening to him that sometimes crime pays so well that it becomes your personal nemesis. You can indeed become a victim of your own success. So the axiom still rings true, "If you can't do the time, don't do the crime."

HONOR SERVICES

I once took a job with forty-two lesbians and me as the only male on the payroll. I didn't plan for it to be that way, but once the dice are rolled you have to play whatever number comes up.

My wife had wearied being a temporary. She worked for an accounting company that sent her out on temporary assignments with various companies. Usually ones that needed help yesterday, but put it off until they were underwater, or so buried in alligators, that in order to save their own jobs the bosses sought emergency help. She seemed to enjoy being needed, so I never interfered with her job choices. Some people like to defuse bombs for a living. There is something about a lit fuse and a bomb in your lap that captures your total attention.

I personally got tired of holding out that I was some kind of miracle man. I lost my taste for pulling burning embers from the fiery furnace and holding them in my bare hands until my skin started peeling off. I saved too many people's jobs only to watch them go on to bigger checks and bigger lies. While I stayed the same, or fell behind. So it was somewhat of a coincidence that we both found ourselves unemployed at the same time. We still had one cub at home with us, so we had the general talk most people have. "Do you want to be the breadwinner, or do you want me to do it?"

We both agreed the cub was old enough that we could both have jobs and still be there at the crucial times. We didn't have a latch key kid with too much time on its hand, with an idle motor running. We both knew that was a sure recipe for trouble. I always defer to my wife in those decisions. Even though I like to think I wear the pants in my family, I let everyone know I wear the pair she tells me to wear. It saves lots of friction and fighting. I know I cannot get between a mother and her cub and come out unscathed, so I never try to. Most men never learn that lesson until they are being repaired in some emergency ward somewhere.

My wife saw the ad first. It said, "Only women wanted."

Now I envisioned naked ladies dancing or porno princesses prancing. Since I knew she wasn't interested in such far flung enterprises, although I think she could learn the trade if the requirement was high enough, and the money was huge enough. I kind of gave it a glance and a snicker. I told her to call them up. It's an illegal ad in the first place. Anyone that's been on the other side of the desk doing the interviewing knows that in America you cannot be that discriminatory in hiring and advertising without inviting the Government to be your partner and constant companion.

She gave them a ring and, lo and behold, they were a candy company. They were looking for lady truck drivers because they had the best work habits, lowest accident records, and were the most consistent and reliable in their comportment.

Well, I was nonplussed to say the least. Since my wife had previously been a semi-truck relief driver with a million mile patch with no tickets or accidents, she decided to go for it. I took her to the address in an industrial park not too far away. She asked for an application and filled it out. Meanwhile, just out of curiosity, I asked the very personable girl at the front desk for an application.

She stutter stepped and said, "We don't hire men so what is the point in your filling out an application? We will just round file it and never call you, so why bother?"

I was bowled over by her sheer audacity and forthrightness. Her candor absolutely unnerved me. Then my testosterone switched on and I went into hyper drive. I believe as closely as I remember I said something like: "Wait a minute, sweetheart, I can do any job a woman can do except have a baby, give me the damn application."

A beautiful Latino girl who appeared not to be paying attention to what we were saying and doing raised her head from her paperwork and said, "Give him an application." all I heard from Shelley the receptionist was, "Yes, maam."

My wife and I went outside to fill out our applications. I had a hard time in deciding what to apply for. I was torn between ruler of the universe, dictator of a small company with the power of life and death over everyone, or janitor.

Anita, the queen bee that all the girls hovered around, came out to interview Linda my wife. She had the rap down cold. The job entailed delivering candy boxes to small businesses in Western Washington. There were seventy-two stops a day. Each box had one hundred items in them. You counted the items. Then you counted the money and you wrote down the amount on the box and replaced the old box with a new one. She had my wife's' interest until she said, "You are responsible for the money and the merchandise. If there is a shortage, it is deducted from your total take at the end of the week. Depending on how much your boxes generate, you can take home some hefty change."

But my wife didn't just parachute into the earth yesterday, nor did she fall off the turnip truck and roll into town. She asked, "What if the customer doesn't pay? They are on their honor to pay but what if they don't?"

Anita never blinked twice. "Then you lose," she said. She was tough and I admired her for that. I found out later she rode and broke horses for other people. She liked to ride her horses and her people hard and put them up sweaty if she could. She kept trying to get Linda to change her mind, but it was to no avail, so she decided to interview me.

I had applied to sell the candy boxes to the end user. She said in a dismissive tone of voice, "We have had some men try this in the past, but they usually burn out real fast when they find out the amount of paperwork involved and the detail required."

I was starting to get a fever for the job. I can smell money no matter how well it is hidden and I smelled money. I only had one question: "Is it a straight commission job, or is there a subsidy?" I have sold tangibles and intangibles for years so it is inconsequential to me whichever I have to sell. I see selling as just sophisticated begging in the first place. It is a means to an end. I don't get dewy eyed about any job. I've been making my own living since I was twelve years old.

Anita explained their pro-rata system of encouragement and compensation. I had to go through a thirty-day probation period. I was introduced to Sandy who would be my trainer and manager. She was married and had lots of personal problems, but I was used to that. In today's dysfunctional world that is the norm, not the exception. I like people with lots of personal problems. They are off center because they don't have control of their lives and they bring it to work with them. They can never get organized and they end up relying on me to make them look good. This means if I can find a way to make more money for the company they don't interfere with me earning ordinary profits while I'm in their employ, that's if you don't get involved in company politics and infighting. I began the job.

They did hire one other guy, but he quit the first day when he sensed which way the wind was blowing. He was a pretty boy. He began with, "Hi, I'm Rick. I'm going to Italy to model guys' clothes. This is just an in between job for me." When he found out none of the women were interested in men or how they looked, he realized he didn't have any leverage, so he quit.

Our trainer gave us the welcome aboard speech. Two girls plus me were the sellers. The two girls were a hoot. One had her personal planner, her cell phone, her diamond tennis bracelet and matching anklet. She was dressed to the nines in Nordstrom clothes. She had on expensive high heels. When we walked into the first industrial park, she had to carry a candy box with a hundred items in it. She had to ask for the boss and sell him on using the service. When we broke for lunch, she kept on walking. We never saw her again. She was a little overdressed and not prepared for toiling in the trenches with the common men and women we ordinarily called upon.

The other girl lasted three weeks. She was a divorced mom with two kids that was trying to get back into the job market. I felt sorry for her and I tried to get her to loosen up and not believe everything she was told, but she was so eager to succeed that when Sandy called sales meetings and didn't show up, it devastated her. When she had a few cancellations and they charged her back from her reserve placement account, it ruined her for keeps.

To my mind the funniest part of working for the company was that my sales manager couldn't sell anything. I never saw her sell a box the whole time I worked for the company, but she liked to do lunch a lot. As long as my quotas were high, she got to drink long lunches. The deal was pretty straightforward. You received three dollars for each box placed until you got to eight boxes, then you got four dollars per box. As soon as you reached twelve boxes you got five dollars per box, so I went for the gold. My first week I placed forty plus boxes, so they made a hold back rule in case my placements were bogus. They held back two dollars per box in a reserve account. Which I was supposed to get at the end of the year as a bonus. I like handicaps; I think it means you're doing something right. Next they demanded I come into the office every morning before beginning my day. Next they demanded I wear a suit and tie. Well, every time they punished me, I punished them back. I sold more boxes, but I became real creative. I made the worker bees buzz. The lesbian truck drivers started having to do pick ups in nudist camps, topless clubs, gambling casinos, gravel quarries, churches, bar and grills, bowling alleys, and lots of other places they hated. They quit trifling with me, so I settled down to making steady money. Steady money is better than quick money. After I placed a hundred and eighty six boxes in one week in Alderwood shopping mall they went nuts. Then they went into a total revolt. They shouldn't have kept telling me nobody ever had successfully done a shopping mall. Security and management wouldn't allow it.

I have always been interested when someone tells me you cannot cook an elephant. You can cook an elephant, but you have to cut it into pieces, and then find a very big pot. Any problem can be cut in half until you find a manageable piece you can work with, then so on until the problem is solved.

When my old man scared the bejesus out of me at twelve years of age telling me I had to earn and pay him six hundred dollars per month or they were taking me back to the orphanage, he taught me the most valuable lesson I ever learned. There is always work to be found. You have to look for it and be flexible. If you keep your fear under control you can earn a decent living. It took three years for Honor Services to learn that I only came to the office in a suit and tie. To me, that is the white man's business uniform. "Hi, I wear a suit and tie so you can trust me." I kept a change of clothes in the trunk of my car. I went to a nearby gas station and changed into Levis and a sweatshirt. I took a picture of the box of goodies on a clipboard. I never let them see what I had on the clipboard until I got the boss and his attention.

My spiel was short and sweet. A real slow pitch. "Hi, I'm from Honor Services; we provide a free courtesy service to businesses in your area." Then I shut up. When he had to break the silence with a question, I explained, "There is no contract we provide the boxes and their contents free of charge to you, but we rely on peoples' sense of fair play to do the right thing and pay for the products they take. Sometimes we lose, but most times we make out okay. We've been doing this for thirteen years. Would you like to try it for a thirty-day test drive and see if it works for you?" The funny thing is, it was one of the funnest jobs I ever had. I got where I could place forty boxes a day in four hours and take the rest of the day off. I learned early that the Parker's law of work was true. i.e. "Work expands to fill the time allotted to it."

I would still be working for them today, but they decided to cheat me on the hold back reserve account. The absentee owner who lived in Minneapolis got tired of flying to Seattle once a month to get a satchel full of money. They had huge cash flow. They had cash counters and coin counters that rivaled any bank. The new owner took control. He was a banker. He knew the first two rules for any company to make a profit are you have to have control of two essential items: cash flow and personnel. He broke up the ladies' club and made the rubber meet the road. I got paid a bucket of money, but I kind of miss the old job and thinking of those ladies having to visit construction sites, hardware stores, nudist camps and all those other places they hated so much.

One last thing…One Easter weekend, when traffic was heavy and even grid locked, one of our drivers had an accident. She called the office crying uncontrollably. She knew Anita fired anyone that had an accident, to keep the company insurance premiums at a minimum. Anita listened quietly for a minute and then in a calm and measured voice said, "Forget all that. Give the guy your insurance information. Be sure and get his and come on in. All that can happen is voices will be raised and words will be said."

It was one of the coolest under fire assessment and examples of damage control I've ever seen. I ranked it right up there with the meeting I attended at Litton Industries when I worked for N.A.S.A. Tex Thorton was told Litton Industries microwave ovens leaked radiation. His response was "How many do we have in inventory? Unload them quickly at discount."

NORTHWEST KINETICS

I had this big friend named Tom; he had way too much energy. He could wear you out just being around him. His mind was like a ricocheting bullet in a tile bathroom. While you were doing one thing with him he was planning three more things to do before the day was out. His frenetic energy wore on everyone around him. We would go to one movie and pay for it then jump from theatre to theatre. Now I was good for about three movies, but Tom wanted to see five, or six, or more back to back. This was a three hundred pound guy. I usually expect big guys to move a little slower than the rest of the public, but not Tom. He would smuggle McDonalds full meals into theatres in his socks, and shorts. You could smell french fries, or freedom fries, if you are a patriot wafting all over the theatre so he would engulf them. In less than five minutes he could wolf down a big and tasty burger, a big mac burger and a fish sandwich with a super size order of fries.

Tom is a human eating machine. I accompanied him once to five Thanksgiving Day dinners. He ate full meals with all the trimmings. I barely got done with the first one. He said he only ate all that food so he wouldn't disappoint the people who invited him.

Every once in awhile I wouldn't hear from Tom for several months. Tom was a real trencherman. Then he would suddenly show up with six of seven things to do the next day, each of them being full time events. Like one day we did the auto show, went to the boat show, toured a time-share, went dancing and then Tom gambled at a casino for four more hours until I was exhausted. It took a few days to recover from our hyper activity, let alone the huge amounts of food ingested. Tom eats fast, and then grabs your food before you can finish it. He hits your front door and goes straight to the refrigerator. His opening words are, "What have you got to eat? I'm starving."

When I haven't seen him for a month or two he always appears leaner and with lots of cash. He wants to go to pawn shops and buy stuff he can sell on the Internet. He has his eighty nine year old mom selling stuff for him on the Internet. One day I asked him where he had been for three months, that I'd called his house for him to go to the sportsman's show and his mom told me he couldn't talk to me or see me for another two weeks. She wouldn't tell me why.

He then unloaded on me. "I'm a drug monkey," he said.

I asked, "What the heck is a drug monkey?"

He explained, "I'm a lab rat, a hamster. You know, a guy the drug companies use to do phase three final drug testing on. They need some humans to get final licensing to sell their drugs to the American public. So I go into their lab for two, or three weeks, or as long as is needed to do their study. I usually lose about thirty to forty pounds. They put you up in this big mansion in Tacoma. You have a dietician that adjusts your menu daily. There are twenty to thirty nurses, big screen televisions, private rooms with maid service, recreation rooms, and beautiful landscaped grounds. You are a prisoner for two, or three weeks but they compensate the hell out of you."

"How? "I asked.

"With money," he said, "paid in cash at the end of the study."

"How much?" I asked.

"It varies with different studies, but it averages a thousand dollars a week."

I got real focused and interested when he said that. "How do I register in their data bank?" I asked.

He told me he would take me in because he got a referral fee if they used me. Now Tom and I occasionally sold our plasma at the blood bank. The first time was good for forty dollars, then they paid you twenty dollars thereafter, but they paid a twenty dollars referral fee. We would load up our car with guys and pick up a few extra bucks occasionally, but nothing like the money he was talking about making. It definitely had my full attention. A week later Tom came to get me and we drove to Tacoma and registered with North West Kinetics for lab testing for large pharmaceutical companies. They took our blood and urine, did chest x rays, gave us the most thorough physical I've ever had, and that includes a flight physical. These guys were very, very, thorough. They had one female doctor that liked to spend an inordinate amount of time testing the sensitivity of our male appendages and associated organs, but it wasn't unpleasant. The meter was running and she seemed to be enjoying that part of the exam so much I certainly didn't want to go against the doctor's orders. They had a lesbian intake nurse that didn't want to talk to the men, but that didn't bother me either. The eighteen blood draws every twenty-four hours, the collecting all your vital fluids, and the .12 lead EKG tests sometimes got onerous, but never so much that I would drop out. You had to stay, sign tons of paperwork that in essence said if they made you into a mutant, or you later gave birth to two headed babies you couldn't sue them or blame them for your subsequent weirdness.

Most of the subjects were women. It was hard to get healthy males to confine themselves for weeks at a time for any amount of money. A lot of the nurses were old warhorses. They had seen it all. Some of the studies you couldn't have visitors for fear they would give you something that would contaminate the data being gathered, like candy bars when we were doing diabetes drug studies, or food when we were doing the Beano study to stop gas and intestinal discomfort. They always did double blind studies. One part of the group received the drug being tested. Another part got a placebo, and a third part took something else. Purportedly, not even the doctors knew which group received the magic elixir. Some of the crap we ate and drank was so noxious that people heaved it up. I felt like a survivor on one of those remote island television shows.

The *Beano* study was my very favorite study. They fed you all the cabbage, cauliflower, rutabaga gas producing stuff you could ingest. We ate beans three meals a day. Well, it quickly became evident which people got the drug. They didn't fart or belch. The rest of us walked around tooting like steam calliopes. You'd be talking to someone and it was like being in a wind tunnel. There was so much farting and belching it's a wonder we didn't inflate that mansion hospital so that it floated away. A lit match would have blown that place right off the map.

The girls would retire to their rooms and let out little squeaker farts. They called it tooting. The men roamed the halls yelling, "Pull my finger," having farting contests and offending the nurses that drew their blood. Finally the doctors called a big meeting and told us to quit being so rude with the staff and each other.

I still received three thousand dollars for three weeks work. All in all, I did eight studies for different drug companies. Some of them may have been flawed, like the one they cut short because a monkey died. The monkey was receiving the proportionate dose of the same medicine we were taking. They still paid us the full amount though. I liked the four thousand dollar study we did for a new blood sugar medication to control diabetes. We were in the second week, when the company told the hospital to discontinue the study. A lab dog's tail fell off. It may have been just a coincidence, but it was good for the full amount for half the time. Some of the women voted to stay on for two more weeks for an additional eighteen hundred dollars. I opted not to. I never checked with anyone to see if any of their appendages fell off, but I decided not to be too greedy.

Sometimes they had several groups in the mansion hospital at the same time. It was most fractious when there would be a normal group. They wanted to stay up all night, have sex with each other, try to score illicit drugs, and any thing else that was disruptive. I learned a lot about my own body and other people's bodies doing these studies. I do believe I helped explore new pathways in explorative medical treatment. I know it's helped me to live a healthier lifestyle than before I did the studies. The pharmaceutical companies paid out a ton of money, and they made land slide profits in return. I personally don't begrudge them a dime. Every once in awhile I'll read something that I was peripherally involved in testing by being a drug monkey and it reassures me there was no harm, no foul. Now if I could just get rid of this strange tumor on my forehead and make my Spock ears and my tail go away, I'd be happy.

417

FAT BOB

There used to be a transmission repair shop in downtown Bellevue. It was kind of surprising because downtown Eighth Street is the main drag. It is the belly of the beast as it were. In the midst of the highest priced real estate in the whole state of Washington was this non-descript scruffy looking, dirty, raggedy, repair facility. I really learned to love that little place and I frequented it regularly. Over the last forty-eight years I have developed a hobby. I find low cost bottom end of the market cars that are run down and need to be restored. I don't run marathons, lift weights, play tennis, or golf. I fix little cars and sell them to people who are in need of cheap transportation. It isn't very lucrative but it is challenging and fun to do.

Every Wednesday the Trans-Tune shop ran a loss leader special ad in the Little Nickel newspaper, a throwaway free paper that comes out once a week all over Washington. For twenty dollars the transmission repair shop would drain the fluid, adjust the transmission if necessary, replace the fluid and the seal and screen. Now this was a steal in today's market with the burgeoning cost of labor in any repair facility. The guy that owned the shop was a little mealy mouthed guy that mumbled and wouldn't look you in the face when he talked to you. He hated my guts because I was always in there having them do my little beater cars. I never bought any extras and I never bought any of their hype about how my car might blow up on the way home, or kill me if I didn't buy a transmission fix immediately.

I've owned a few cars in forty-eight years. I don't get dewey eyed about anything that can be bought for money. I kid people that ask me if I ever had children of my own by telling them "Yes, but I sold them for medical experiments." It stops that line of inquiry.

The other reason Dwayne hated me so bad was I supervised them with an eagle eye and an implacable heart. I made them do their work right, or I made them do it over and I wouldn't leave the premises until it was finished correctly no matter how long it took. I never was in a hurry. Well, one day after fifteen years of exploiting their facility to the max, I had the shock of my life. Dwayne had hired a five hundred fifty pound guy in Osh Kosh can't bust em coveralls that called himself "Fat Bob'! He was from Mississippi and he let his southern drawl and good ole boy ways disarm people while he figured out which way to screw them. He was truly menacing. Now, I have known some pretty heavy dudes in my time. But very few seem deadly. Most fat guys seem relatively harmless. For some reason an angry Santa Claus just doesn't seem very lethal. Even Sumo wrestlers with all their bulk and size don't seem like likely candidates for contract killers, but Fat Bob was an exception to that rule. His slitted eyes and that slow drawl of his felt like a big bull alligator slipping up on you. Well, the rules changed dramatically in ye old friendly trans repair shop. Dwayne no longer greeted the customers. He didn't stare at the floor and write up the work order. Fat Bob took over and if you left out any wording to an implied meaning, it ended up costing you extra, especially, if you were a woman. I saw women bring cars in and the license plates, the carburetors, drive shafts, or anything else Bob fancied, would disappear within an hour of dropping their cars off. When they would come back to retrieve their cars, tears, shouting, swearing and threats would ensue, but all it got was the wrath of Fat Bob directed with all his five hundred fifty pounds of force pointed at them. He impounded their cars until they paid the bill. The small print on the contract had a disclaimer that said, "All cars are parked in an unsecured area behind the facility and the business and management were not responsible for any loss or damage to the customer's vehicle." I watched Bob and Dwayne increase their profits over six thousand percent over the next three years. No one was able to stop them or shut them down. Although numerous complaints were filed against them, the Chamber of Commerce quit taking complaints because their files were overflowing from the ones they already had on file. The police were helpless to act because the disclaimer covered the bases of technical legality. Bob and Dwayne tried hard to discourage me from coming in any more, but as long as they ran their coupon ad I was determined to cash in on it. They insulted me, calling me a user, a parasite, a sponge, and a free loader. I cheerfully agreed with all those descriptions. You can't chase a starving man away from a free picnic or a barbecue.

Well, the day of my come-uppance finally arrived. I met a master mechanic named Ian. He bought little cars at the auto auction. They usually needed serious mechanical attention or major bodywork. Ian did both. He even did it at home. He had a complete repair facility built onto his home. He was also smog certified. He could do just about anything. I haunted his place whenever I needed a car. In so doing, I discovered a custom 1986 Oldsmobile Cutlass Supreme Broughm. It was black with red velour interior. It was perfect in every respect but one. Somebody T-boned it from the side in an intersection and the rear door was caved in.

I made the mistake of showing the car to my wife. She fell in love with it immediately. She wanted me to sell both our little beater cars we were driving and buy her that car. Ian and I punched each other's dance card and began to waltz each other around the arena over that car. We finally struck a deal at four hundred fifty dollars, which was a ton of money to me at the time.

We bought the car and I took it to Trans-Tune to have the transmission refreshed. Fat Bob was friendly, affable and funny. He joked with all the customers. He and Dwayne had been drinking all morning. It was a hot summer day. I found out Dwayne was a closet alcoholic. Two beers and mild mannered Clark Kent became Mr. Hyde. Bob had to keep Dwayne in the back of the shop because he was using profanity, cursing the customers and in general making a horse's ass out of himself. I was genuinely amazed. I had never seen such a profound personality change with just two beers. I found out that Bob and Dwayne had just formed a partnership. Bob was now the driving influence and Dwayne was the silent partner. I'm afraid while Dwayne was out plowing the south forty acres he sold his farm to Bob, as they say down South. The tail was wagging the dog. Bob cheerfully serviced my wifes new car. He took my coupon and thanked me for my business. Then he set the hook. When my wife came to get the car he asked her how much she paid for it? She told him four hundred fifty dollars. He wiped his brow and exclaimed, "Boy you stole this baby."

Meanwhile, Ian had fixed every thing externally, but warned us he heard some lower bearing noise in the engine. He duly warned us, "It may go a year, or a day. Eventually you will need to do the engine to keep the car forever."

As my wife prepared to leave, Bob said, "Linda for four hundred fifty dollars, I'll completely rebuild your engine to original factory specifications and I'll completely restore your transmission to factory specs. You will then have a four thousand dollar car.

I asked how he could do it so cheaply? Everyone else wanted five thousand five hundred dollars to do the transmission and engine. He told us he sponsored a racecar east of the mountains, lived in the governors old mansion in Olympia and he had two more transmission shops, that he was a lot more successful than he appeared to be, or than we ever imagined. I must admit we were totally surprised. We went home and talked about it.

Linda was invited to Ohio to her Dad's new marriage, so she went and left the car and half the money for parts up front with Big Bob. It was supposed to be done in one week. Well, the rest is just a nightmare we will both never forget in ten lifetimes. Fat Bob lied: thirty-nine weeks later the plates, the carb, the tranny, the engine, and anything else of value including the new Sears diehard battery had disappeared. We tried every recourse without relief. We begged, we cajoled, we whined, we sniveled, we threatened, but nothing worked.

Now in prison if you sell a wolf ticket to someone, it means you convince them you are the big bad wolf and you are going to blow their house down, or eat their face for a dime. I don't sell wolf tickets, but we went to get our car back. When we got there Bob was in a very foul mood. He met us at the door and told us to get off his property or he would have us both arrested or killed. He told us. "I killed a man in Mississippi and never served a day in jail."

I believed him, but when he told me get your bitch off my lot, or I will, he went a little too far. Linda was a semi truck relief driver before I met her. She had a million mile patch with no tickets or accidents. I had seen a semi truck idling next door to Bobs when we drove up, but it didn't have any significance for me. When Bob went into his office I saw Linda go towards the idling Semi truck and I knew Fat Bob was going to be turned into a fly in the grill or a hood ornament on that truck. I went into the office to get him out of there before an act of vengeance and a righteous anger took their toll on him. He thought I came to attack him. He jumped up from his desk yelling that I was a dead man. I knew that in a few seconds I'd hear a diesel engine revving up and the gears grinding into place. I explained he had less than thirty seconds to live, that five hundred fifty pounds and can't bust em coveralls couldn't save him from an eighty thousand pound speeding diesel truck. I got him outside. I talked my angry wife into going to the car. She finally acquiesced, but she didn't want to. This was no longer just about the car. Bob threatened to drag me out back and kill me like he had done other guys. I explained that things are often not as they appear to be in this life. Kindness is often mistaken for weakness. I also explained that we were having our car towed away, that I would deal with him on a more personal level. I stayed alert and focused while I talked to Bob. I watched his hands very carefully. And I never lost sight of the third button down on his chest. Three buttons down on any man's shirt and you stop their heart with one well-placed blow. There are only two ways to die. Your heart stops beating and you quit breathing. I was tempted for Fat Bob to have a sudden inexplicable accident out behind his facility, but I thought of a better way. I walked away.

Then we filled out the obligatory police report. We also filed an insurance claim. We then looked Bob, and Dwayne up on the Internet. We filed U.C.C. filings against their corporations, their joint property and all their personal property. My insurance agent had a wife from a third world country. He had her working for free in his office. He ordered her around like an indentured servant. He told her to refuse our claim. I went to the claims supervisor for the company. She overrode him. I asked her to replace the car with one of like value, or pay money. They had us sign off on the claim. They then paid us thirty three hundred dollars. There was no other car like it in their system.

They then prosecuted Bob and Dwayne. They found thirty-seven mini storage lockers full of stolen car parts. Bob and Dwayne are now in prison. I sued them civilly in small claims court, got a judgment and was paid. Sometimes the little guy does win.

Like I said in the beginning of this report. "There used to be a transmission repair shop in the heart of downtown Bellevue, but not any more. When I started this book it was to expose true criminals that I have encountered in my short lifetime, but I rue the fact that they cannot all be apprehended and brought to justice. I've read that it is written there is a temporary law of suspended justice upon the earth right now...but one day it will be lifted. When that day occurs, whether a just God judges us and metes out divine punishment, or we judge ourselves, I am convinced that evil will fail and the right will prevail. To this end I dedicate my heart and will and I hope you do to.

GLOSSARY

Baddest	Most ruthless
Bell	Dispatched call
Chicken Meat	Under aged children
Crash	Sleep when exhausted
Cub	Child under 18
Dempsey Dumpster	Garbage container
Dyke	Aggressive homosexual female
Fall	Downfall
Fall partner	Someone convicted with you
Flatten your sentence	Do all the time, no parole or probation
Fronting	Pay money for someone else: Present an acceptable appearance
Ghost	An erased computer file
Grand Mal	Large convulsion
Grapevine	Communication network
Hooked up	Handcuffed, connected

Hooking up	Handcuffing, joining with someone else
Ice	Kill someone
Jacket	Crime you are charged with: reputation
Juice	Connections or influence
Kite	A written note
Latch Key Kid	A kid with a key to the house they live in
Loping Dog	Greyhound bus
Monty Hall	Let's make a deal
Patted Down	To search your person for weapons
Pederast	Sexual deviant that preys on children
Prozac/Paxil	Prescribed tranquilizers
Psyched	Deceived
Quaaludes	A prescription tranquilizer
Rap	Story
Reached out	Called a favor
Scripts	A doctors prescription
Short eyes	Someone who sees children

	as prey
Stash	Drug supply
Stoked	Pumped, excited
Stones	Testicles
Strung Out	Drugged
Tagged Out	Arrested or Killed
The Dragon	Heroin
Toked	Inhaling marijuana smoke
Wasted	Drugged or Killed
Whacked	Killed or dysfunctional
Wolf Ticket	Imminent threat to harm someone
Pruno	Prunes and yeast fermented in a garbage bag.

ABOUT THE AUTHOR

Lamont Cranston is a Native American born on the reservation in Kalispell, Montana. He now lives in Seattle, Washington with his wife Linda and a Shit-Tzsu puppy named Simba.

Cranston served in the military in the United States Air Force. He has a cryptography clearance and worked at SAC headquarters in Omaha, Nebraska. His formal education was accomplished in Hawaii, Madison Wisconsin, and Provo Utah.

Lamont was voted International Poet of the year 1999. Other books by Lamont Cranston are:

"Star Worlds" A comparative analysis of Ancient Manuscripts.

"Whimsical Tales" A collection of seventeen original short stories with embedded morals hidden in them. Some of the stories are true stories. The reader is challenged to find out which stories are true?

"True Stories From Seattle" A compendium of malefactors. Their crimes, the dates, where, and how they were committed.

CPSIA information can be obtained at www.ICGtesting.com
Printed in the USA
LVOW121030050613

337070LV00001B/3/P